INTERVENTION: Science of Reading

Ways to Say Long /a/

Phonics for Older Struggling Readers

© Two Pencils and a Book
Information: https://www.teacherspayteachers.com/Store/Two-Pencils-And-A-Book
Long A – Ways to Say Long A - Basic Phonics for Literacy - Science of Reading - For Older Struggling Readers

ISBN - 979-8329449938

Table of Contents

Table of Contents

The Science of Reading

Effective Literacy Instruction for Older Struggling Readers

Research is clear, for effective literacy instruction, practice is needed in phonological awareness, phonics and word recognition, fluency, vocabulary and oral language comprehension, and text comprehension.

Phonological Awareness: Teach students to recognize and manipulate sounds within words, moving from syllables to individual phonemes. Explicitly connect phonemes to letters to support word decoding. Orthographic processing—acquiring, storing, and using letters and letter patterns—is essential for reading instruction.

Phonics and Word Recognition: Explicitly and systematically teach letter sounds and sound-spelling patterns. Practice reading and writing words in isolation and within text is imperative.

Fluency: Provide frequent opportunities for students to read and re-read orally from connected text, including sentences, paragraphs, and passages. Focus on developing both automatic word recognition and fluent expression, with an emphasis on understanding the text.

Vocabulary and Oral Language Comprehension: Incorporate high-quality, language-rich interactions in instruction. Ensure students know what words mean and how to pronounce them.

Comprehension: Teach students to use metacognitive strategies such as setting a purpose, monitoring for meaning, making inferences, and recalling text.

Research Based

Why Fluency?

To be considered "on level" in reading fluency, students should be able to read aloud an unrehearsed passage, (i.e., either narrative or expository, fiction or non-fiction that is 150 to 300 words in length) from a grade-level text, with at least 95% accuracy in word reading. As students read aloud, their reading should sound as effortless as if they were speaking (Hasbrouck & Glaser, 2012.) This does not come easily for some students, which is why fluency practice is so essential.

In order to be considered fluent readers, students in grades 9 through 12 should be able to correctly read 150 words per minute (Hasbrouck & Tindal, 2006). In 2006 and again in 2010, Hasbrouck and Hasbrouck and Tindal (respectively) put forth that "[i]t is sufficient for students to read unpracticed, grade-level text at the 50th percentile of oral reading fluency norms" and that "...teachers do not need to have students read faster because there is no evidence that reading faster than the 50th percentile increases comprehension." See chart below.

The best strategy for developing and improving reading fluency is to provide students with opportunities to read the same passages orally several times. These exercises provide such opportunities. On each passage, there is space for reading fluency calculations. The best part is that the passages are quick and make it easy for students to read aloud repeatedly – and often – without taking up a lot of valuable classroom time. The activities can also be spread over several days.

In an updated 2017 study, Hasbrouck & Tindal reported that "students scoring 10 or more words below the 50th percentile using the average score of two unpracticed readings from grade-level materials need a fluency-building program. Teachers can also use the table to set long-term fluency goals for struggling readers."

Research suggests that one of the easiest and most effective ways for teachers to address reading fluency is to implement quick timed fluency into their weekly schedules.

Grade	Percentile	Fall WPM	Winter WPM	Spring WPM		Grade	Percentile	Fall WPM	Winter WPM	Spring WPM
1	90		81	111		5	90	166	182	194
	75		47	82			75	139	156	168
	50		23	53			50	110	127	139
	25		12	28			25	85	99	109
	10		6	15			10	61	74	83
2	90	106	125	142		6	90	177	195	204
	75	79	100	117			75	153	167	177
	50	51	72	89			50	127	140	150
	25	25	42	61			25	98	111	122
	10	11	18	31			10	68	82	93
3	90	128	146	162		7	90	180	192	202
	75	99	120	137			75	156	165	177
	50	71	92	107			50	128	136	150
	25	44	62	78			25	102	109	123
	10	21	36	48			10	79	88	98
4	90	145	156	180		8-12	90	185	199	199
	75	119	139	152			75	161	173	177
	50	94	112	123			50	133	146	151
	25	68	87	98			25	106	115	125
	10	45	61	72			10	77	84	97

This is an evidence-based program, and it works.

Begin each passage as a guided reading. This is an evidence-based strategy for improving reading fluency. The student is asked to read the same passage three to five times, receiving feedback each time from the instructor or peer reviewer. Feedback comes from peers or instructors – using the Fluency templates. By providing feedback on accuracy, rate and expression, students can incorporate those changes into each subsequent reading, eventually reaching a point of fluency with that particular passage. They can then move on to more difficult assignments.

Repeated readings of text can also contribute to better comprehension, one of the cornerstones of reading throughout life. All schools, from elementary to college, can easily provide students with repeated readings as well as paired passages of the same theme or topic.

For those teachers who want to mix-up full-class fluency lessons, one option is fluency-oriented reading instruction (FORI). This evidence-based practice begins with a teacher reading a particular passage aloud while students follow along in silent reading. Then, students read the passage aloud numerous times throughout the week, including echo, choral and partner reading. They also practice the passage for 15-30 minutes daily. At the end of a week, students engage in discussion, writing an essay or performing other activities that prove comprehension of the passage.

Reading Level Conversion Chart

Grade	F&P	Lexile	DRA	ATOS
Kindergarten	A	BR0L	1	0.1
Kindergarten	B	50L	2	1
Kindergarten	C	75L	4	1.2
1st Grade	D	100L	6	1.3
1st Grade	E	150L	8	1.5
1st Grade	F	175L	10	1.7
1st Grade	G	200L	12	1.8
2nd Grade	H	250L	14	2.1
2nd Grade	I	275L	16	2.2
2nd Grade	J	325L	18	2.4
2nd Grade	K	375L	20	2.7
3rd Grade	L	425L	24	3
3rd Grade	M	475L	28	3.2
3rd Grade	N	575L	30	3.8
4th Grade	O	625L	34	4.1
4th Grade	P	675L	38	4.4
5th Grade	Q	725L	40	4.7
5th Grade	R	775L	40	5
6th Grade	S	825L	40	5.3
6th Grade	T	875L	50	5.7
7th Grade	U	925L	50	6.1
8th Grade	V	975L	50	6.5
9th Grade	W	1025L	60	7
10th Grade	X	1050L	60	7.2
11th Grade	Y	1075L	70	7.5
12th Grade	Z	1100L	80	7.8

How to Complete Fluency Exercises

This program works for resource, whole class, RTI, and summer school. The progress monitoring page allows for tracking. If you are using this program with more than one student – partner up. Partnering students is engaging and lets everyone participate. I find that students helping students builds confidence and reinforces learning; additionally, by reading, tracking and reading again, student exposure to each passage is maximized. Research suggests that pairing readings with like-level reading partners is motivating and increases reading success.

INSTRUCTIONS AND SCRIPT

Before you begin, have a copy of one passage for each student. The PDF can be displayed before the whole class on a Smartboard or printed and projected on a document camera. As you explain the lessons, demonstrate what students will be doing.

Explain what fluency is - the rate and ease at which we read along with the flow of reading.

About breaking students into pairs. If you are working with a group of students with varying abilities - pair like-leveled students together.

Explain the entire activity, as well as how to calculate combined words per minute, or CWPM. Then read the passage aloud. Have students track on their pages as you read aloud. It is extremely beneficial for struggling students to hear the passage before they read it aloud. The goal isn't to have students stumble, but to optimize opportunities for ultimate success.

The first few times you do fluency as a class – the script below may be helpful:

1. **Check to make sure each person is in the right spot and then read the passage.**
2. **After you read the selected passage aloud, partner students and say something like:** *Put your name on your paper. Since you need to be marking your partner's paper, switch papers now. Raise your hand if you are Partner 1.*
3. **Pause until one student from each pair has their hand raised – acknowledge students when one person of each pair has their hand raised.**
4. **Raise your hand if you are Partner 2.** Pause until the other student from each pair has their hand raised – acknowledge students when the other partner has their hand raised.

    Excellent. When I say "Begin", all Partner 1s should quietly begin to read to their partners.

    All Partner 2s will use their pencils to keep track of their partner's errors. Partner 2s will put a line over each word pronounced incorrectly.

    When the timer goes off, all Partner 2s will circle the last word read, but Partner 1s will keep reading until the passage is complete. Does anyone have any questions?

5. **Set the timer for one minute. If there are no questions -** *Begin.*
6. **When the timer goes off give time for students to finish:** *Partner 2s, please mark your partner's score and give feedback to Partner 1s. To calculate CWPM subtract the number of errors from the total number of words read.*
7. **Walk around the room to make sure scores are being marked correctly.**
8. **Make sure students are ready and then switch for Partner 2s to read.**

    Ready? Begin.

Remember the science of reading is an ever-evolving approach to teaching. It is research that guides reading instruction and phonics and phonemic awareness is a big part of it – so is fluency and comprehension. This resource embodies the SOR approach. Now to Long A.

The long A sound can be spelled using 8 different patterns:

- The most common spellings of long /ā/ are **A, A-E, AI,** and **AY.**
- Less frequent ways to spell /ā/ are **EI, EA, EIGH,** and **EY.**

These patterns can be heard at the beginning, middle, or end of words. Long /ā/ can be spelled with a <u>silent e</u>, <u>open syllable</u>, or using a vowel team.

1. a like **a**corn
2. a-e like t**a**k**e**
3. ai like r**ai**n
4. ay like s**ay**
5. ei like r**ei**ndeer
6. ea like st**ea**k
7. eigh like **eigh**t
8. ey like h**ey**

Tips For Teaching The Long A Sound and Spelling FYI

When you start teaching long a, focus on spelling generalizations. Teach one spelling pattern at a time, and once one is mastered you can add in another. It's much easier to learn how to read these patterns than to learn how to spell them. Since they all sound the same and can appear in the same place, choosing the right spelling pattern can be tricky.

Teach the process for deciding on the spelling pattern.

Once students are familiar with all the options for spelling long a and they know open syllables and the silent e syllable, you can teach them the process for determining the spelling pattern a word has.

When students come across a word with long a and they need to figure out which spelling pattern to choose, here are the questions they can ask:

1. Is there more than one syllable?

2. Is there a base word?

3. Where is the long a sound in the word?

4. Could this be one of those rare spelling options

Which Long A to Use?

When you come across a word with LONG A and you need to figure out which spelling pattern to choose, here are the questions you can ask:

1. Is there more than one syllable?

2. Is there a base word?

3. Where is the long a sound in the word?

4. Could this be one of those rare spelling options

Syllable Review

All all words are made up of syllables.

Syllables come in patterns.

Syllable patterns are the repeating ways sounds are put together to make words.

These patterns help us understand how words are made and pronounced. Syllable division rules are guidelines that show us how to split words into syllables. There are some basic rules for dividing words.

CVC words (consonant-vowel-consonant) and VC/V words (vowel-consonant/vowel) are common patterns taught in early reading lessons. For example, "cat," "dog," and "pen" follow the CVC pattern, with a consonant at the beginning and end and a vowel in the middle. Words like "at," "up," and "it" are VC/V words, having a consonant at only one end. This involves open syllables.

There are also "team" and "blend" patterns. A team of two vowels can make one sound, as in "bean" or "boat." Two consonants can also blend together, without a vowel in between, like in "track" or "ship." In "ship," the /sh/ combination is a consonant digraph, where two consonants make one sound. Common digraphs include /ch/, /sh/, and /th/.

There are several common syllable division rules to teach students how to find open and closed syllables. These rules help students understand and pronounce words correctly.

The 6 Types of Syllables

1. **Closed Syllables** Closed syllables have a short vowel sound and are surrounded by consonants. These words can have one or more syllables. Examples of one-syllable closed syllable words are "cat," "bed," and "stuff." CVC words like "cat" and "bed" have a consonant-vowel-consonant pattern and a short vowel sound between two consonants. Multisyllabic examples include "napkin," "picnic," and "magnet."

2. **Open Syllables** Open syllables end with a long vowel sound and are spelled with a single vowel, usually without a consonant. Examples of open syllables are "I," "a," "go," and "open." The vowel stands alone or is not attached to other vowels.

3. **Vowel-Consonant-e Syllables** Vowel-consonant-e words, also called VCe words, end with a silent "e" that makes the previous vowel a long vowel. This is often called the "magic e" in teaching. Examples are "bike," "gate," and "fine." You can show students how adding a silent "e" to CVC words changes the vowel sound, turning "mop" into "mope."

4. **Vowel Team Syllables** Vowel team syllables have two vowels working together to make one sound, known as diphthongs or vowel digraphs. The vowels can be different letters. Examples are "boat," "moon," and "eight."

5. **Consonant-le Syllables** Consonant-le syllables don't have a vowel sound and come at the end of longer words. They are the last syllable and end with a consonant followed by "le" or its variations like "cle," "dle," "fle," "gle," "ple," "ble." The silent "e" at the end affects the pronunciation. Examples are "table," "purple," and "turtle."

6. **R-controlled Syllables** An r-controlled syllable has one vowel followed by "r," making a unique sound. These are called "bossy r" words because the "r" changes how the vowel sounds. Examples are "bird," "barn," and "fern."

Phonics for Older Students

Long /ā/

Two Pencils and a Book

Open Syllable Words

The letter A will say its name, or its long sound, when it is the last letter in a syllable.

This is called an open syllable.

Open syllables are an important part of learning about words and sounds. An open syllable has a long vowel sound and only has a consonant sound on one side of the vowel, not both. Because there is no consonant closing the vowel sound, the vowel can be pronounced longer.

For example, the words "me" and "go" are open-syllable words. In "me," the open syllable has one vowel that makes a long /ē/ sound. In "go," the open syllable has one vowel at the end, making a long vowel sound.

Understanding open syllables helps us see how syllables work together to make different types of words, like closed syllables and longer words. For instance, the open-syllable word "me" can be joined with other syllables to make words like "meet" or "mean." Similarly, "go" can be joined with other syllables to make words like "got" or "goal." Teaching students to spot open and closed syllables helps them break down and pronounce words more accurately.

<u>Direction for Presentation:</u> To practice - Work through the Google Slide Presentation at this link. There is also a PDF of the presentation and individual PNGs of each slide. Explain Long a and open syllables. Project the slide, have students write the word. Have students divide the word into syllables and either underline or circle the Long a sound.

https://docs.google.com/presentation/d/1kgos89wVPt3Nyz4xxlndWSVZBIHIBsO8wtNKUyZYs48/edit?usp=sharing

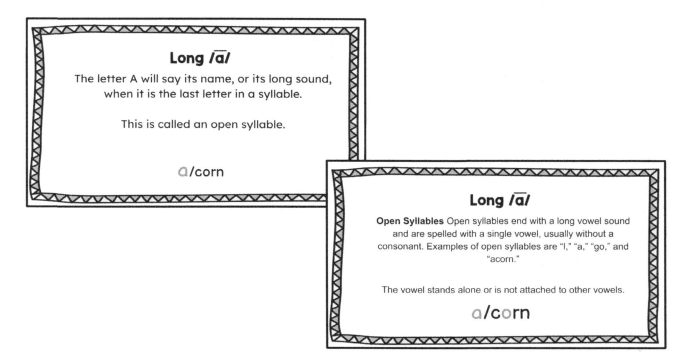

Name: _____ Number: _____

Test Date 1: _____ Test Date 2: _____

Long A = /ā/
Teacher Page

Teacher Say: Put your finger on the first word. We are going to read down the column. Read each word. Begin.

Word	Correct	Word	Correct
acorn		potato	
able		crazy	
bacon		basic	
baby		favor	
paper		labor	
lady		basis	
station		acre	
radio		angel	
famous		Amy	
major		native	
taste		paste	
maple		mason	
waste		alien	
Asia		data	
nation		fatal	

Name: _____ Number: _____

Test Date 1: _____ Test Date 2: _____

Long A = /ā/

Student Page

Word	Word
acorn	potato
able	crazy
bacon	basic
baby	favor
paper	labor
lady	basis
station	acre
radio	angel
famous	Amy
major	native
taste	paste
maple	mason
waste	alien
Asia	data
nation	fatal

Long a – List One

Directions: Read each word three times. Shade in a triangle each time you read. △ △ △

acorn	able	bacon	baby	paper
lady	station	radio	famous	major
taste	maple	waste	Asia	nation

Directions: Underline the long a. Write each word four times.

acorn				
able				
bacon				
baby				
paper				
lady				
station				
radio				
famous				
major				
taste				
maple				
waste				
Asia				
nation				

Name: _____ Number: _____

Long a

Directions: Read the sentences three times each. Shade in a triangle after each read. △ △ △

1. The acorn fell from the tree.
2. Are you able to go home?
3. I love brown bacon.
4. The baby was funny.
5. Pass me the yellow paper.
6. The lady held the baby.
7. Take me to the station.
8. Turn on the radio.
9. The actor was famous.
10. I have a major pimple.
11. Taste the cookie and, tell me if it is good.
12. Don't waste the cookies.
13. China is in Asia.
14. China is a nation in Asia.

Directions: Write four sentences using the long a words from List One.

1. _____

_____

2. _____

_____

3. _____

_____

4. _____

_____

Long a - One

"Pick up the acorns." Amy said. "We will make a paste. We'll run them in water. We'll	17
make the acorns with bacon."	22
"Yeck!" Ray said. "Acorns have to be run under water. They have to be run under a	39
lot of water."	42
"We are able to do that. The lady said they taste so good. The lady said they taste	60
so good with maple syrup," Amy said. "We'll make acorn pancakes."	71
"You have to run them under water for 30 minutes. Then you have to mash them	87
up," Ray said.	90
"I know," Amy said. "Here. Hold the baby. I'll do the acorns."	102
"Okay," said Ray. "I was able to pick up lots of acorns. You make it. I'll try it."	120
"I'll use my famous pancake recipe. I'll start the bacon after I do the acorns."	135

Words Read:	Words Read:	Words Read:
minus mistakes:	minus mistakes:	minus mistakes:
equals wpms:	equals wpms:	equals wpms:

1. What is Amy making? _____

2. What is the main idea of the reading? _____
_____
_____

3. Write two details that support the main idea. _____
_____
_____
_____

4. Write one sentence to finish the reading? _____
_____
_____

Name: _____ Number: _____

Long a – Cloze Reading

Directions: Fill in the blanks with the correct long a word. Words may be used more than once.

"What _____ are you going to?" Jay asked.

"I'm going to Asia," Amy said.

"_____ is not a nation. It's a continent," Jay said.

"I know that. I'm going to China. Then I'm going to Japan. I'm taking the baby to meet

her grandma. You just said nation. I call it a country. I don't really say nation." Amy said.

"That's a _____ trip," Jay said. "Do you need a ride to the station? What time do

you have to be there?"

"Hand me that paper," Amy said. "The times are on the _____." Jay handed

Amy the paper. "I have to be there at one. I'm meeting a lady with the group."

"I can get you to the _____ by one. We can eat before," Jay said.

"Maple bars. Let's get the maple bars with bacon. That's great to eat before I go," Amy

said.

"Okay. We'll bring food for the _____. The baby shouldn't have maple bars. We'll

get the _____ bars with _____. Then we'll go to the station," Jay said.

"Then off to Asia!" Amy said.

"Then off to Asia," Jay said. "I'm so glad you're _____ to go."

"Me too. I can't wait to see the baby's grandma. I can't wait to _____ the food. I

can't wait to go to Asia," Amy said.

"You'll be there soon."

Word Bank				
maple	baby	bacon	Asia	taste
able	station	major	nation	paper

Long a – List Two

Directions: Read each word three times. Shade in a triangle each time you read. △△△

potato	crazy	basic	favor	labor
basis	acre	angel	Amy	native
paste	mason	alien	data	fatal

Directions: Underline the long a. Write each word four times.

potato				
crazy				
basic				
favor				
labor				
basis				
acre				
angel				
Amy				
native				
paste				
mason				
alien				
data				
fatal				

Name: _____ Number: _____

Long a

Directions: Read the sentences three times each. Shade in a triangle after each read. △ △ △

1. Do me a favor and eat the potato.
2. They went crazy for the maple bars.
3. He can do basic math.
4. The mistake was fatal.
5. The workers did the labor.
6. What is the basis of your work?
7. We live on one acre.
8. The angel had wings.
9. Amy ate the baked potato.
10. The plant is native to the park.
11. Paste the paper to the wood.
12. Put the jam in a Mason jar.
13. The alien flew to space.
14. The date shows we won.

Directions: Write four sentences using the long a words above.

1. _____

_____

2. _____

_____

3. _____

_____

4. _____

_____

Long a - Two

John was having dinner with Amy. He was telling her about his farm.	13
"It's basic," John said. "I can plant a potato crop. I can plant a potato crop on my	31
acre."	32
"You are going to need help. You can't do all of the labor yourself," Amy said.	48
"I can do the labor. It's only an acre. I have data on how much labor is needed."	66
John was an Idaho native. He grew up growing potatoes. He'd labored before.	79
"You're crazy to do all of the labor. You'll be working all the time. What's the basis	84
of your data?" Amy asked.	89
"A book" John said. "Do me a favor, trust me on this." John handed Amy some	105
soda. It was in a Mason jar. "A little labor won't be fatal."	118
"Thanks," she said. She took the Mason jar. "Or a lot of labor."	131
"Or a lot of labor," John said.	138
"I can't wait to see this," Amy said.	146
"I can't wait to taste the potatoes," John said. "Dinner's ready. Let's eat."	159

Words Read:	Words Read:	Words Read:
minus mistakes:	minus mistakes:	minus mistakes:
equals wpms:	equals wpms:	equals wpms:

1. What is John going to do? _____

2. What is the main idea of the reading? _____
_____
_____

3. Write two details that support the main idea. _____
_____
_____
_____

4. Write one sentence to finish the reading? _____
_____
_____

Name: _____ Number: _____

Long a – Cloze Reading

Directions: Fill in the blanks with the correct long a word. Words may be used more than once.

"Do me a favor," said Jay. "Do me a favor and pass the last potato."

"Okay. Be an angel. Be an _____, and paste the label on the Mason jar," Amy said.

"The alien label?" Jay asked. He ate the last potato. He pasted the label on the _____ jar.

"Yes, they're for the party," Amy said. "Tess loves _____."

"It's crazy! Tess is twelve already."

"It is crazy. She was just a _____," Amy said. "Now, she's basically a teen."

"Where's the party this year?" Jay asked.

"Tess wants it at Alien Acres," Amy said.

Alien _____ was a farm. It used to be a _____ farm. Now it's a park. People used to go there to see aliens at night.

"Have you seen the _____ on that place?" Jay asked. "There have been four fatal alien landings."

"Not true," Amy said. "That's a rumor spread by a crazy lady. There is no basis of truth in it at all."

"I don't know," Jay said. "Real data is the _____ of the rumor."

"Just _____ labels. We'll worry about aliens later," Amy laughed. "Fatal alien landings," she said to herself. "You're the one who is _____."

Jay laughed too.

Word Bank				
angel	Mason	aliens	baby	potato
acres	data	basis	crazy	paste

Name: _____ Number: _____

Long a Word Search

Directions: Find the long a words. The words can be up or down, left to right, or diagonal.

```
T  A  C  O  R  N  H  E  M  D  A  I  L  A  B  O  R  N
S  B  A  C  O  N  A  F  F  A  M  O  U  S  M  I  C  R
A  L  O  N  D  E  R  N  A  T  I  V  E  S  C  W  A  P
Y  E  G  R  A  D  I  O  D  A  M  Y  N  K  T  A  D  T
S  O  M  E  M  A  S  O  N  B  O  B  A  B  Y  S  A  A
T  F  C  R  A  Z  Y  I  P  O  T  A  T  O  E  T  U  S
A  C  R  E  S  W  I  M  A  S  F  S  I  L  A  E  G  T
T  H  E  N  I  N  D  Y  P  G  I  I  O  T  R  I  H  E
I  Q  A  L  A  D  Y  E  E  I  F  C  N  A  S  K  T  T
O  A  D  B  O  R  N  L  R  S  T  A  Y  P  A  S  T  E
N  D  F  A  V  O  R  L  E  A  N  G  E  L  I  K  E  S
Y  O  U  S  O  M  E  O  A  M  I  C  H  E  L  L  E  M
U  A  L  I  E  N  F  W  D  Y  E  A  R  M  A  P  L  E
I  N  N  S  T  A  Y  S  S  D  G  M  A  J  O  R  O  M
```

Word Bank

acorn	potato	baby	favor	station	acre	major	native
able	crazy	paper	labor	radio	angel	taste	paste
bacon	basic	lady	basis	famous	Amy	maple	mason
	Asia	nation	alien	data	waste	fatal	

Long A Word Maze

Directions: Follow the LONG A words to the END. You may move up and down or left and right.

START	rain	main	play	day	may	pay
acorn	bay	faithful	way	ray	say	clay
able	pray	rainy	display	sleep	agree	guarantee
bacon	aim	maintain	today	display	array	today
potato	sleep	delay	relay	holiday	essay	betrayal
crazy	basic	Asia	baby	employee	steep	queen
waiting	plainly	domain	paper	pray	saying	display
breeze	payable	may	lady	read	bread	breed
feed	labor	favor	nation	zookeeper	volunteer	employee
degree	basis	guarantee	draining	exclaim	peace	peaceful
feature	alien	teenager	clean	frail	beneath	decrease
reason	radio	season	engineer	raisin	see	tree
famous	station	season	reason	attain	teach	creature
data	queen	beaver	degree	paint	contain	waitress
acre	freeze	overseen	cheer	beneath	beach	rain
angel	waste	major	taste	maple	paste	END

Circle the Long A Words

Directions: Circle the Long A words.

acorn	bread	breed	the	mason	time	Asia
able	when	fatal	where	were	hog	native
dog	baby	cat	paste	crazy	dog	queen
paper	tree	out	round	ground	mouth	dog
about	loud	able	loudmouth	pound	nation	mount
account	astound	doubt	maple	doubtful	aloud	bouncy
crazy	amount	recount	thousand	grew	favor	log
grew	crew	chew	flew	drew	stew	knew
famous	dew	view	blew	bacon	brew	new
threw	basic	news	labor	cashew	jewelry	Preview
nephew	review	basis	preview	interview	curfew	potato
sigh	high	thigh	light	alien	something	green
red	station	blue	flight	night	might	right
data	sight	tight	radio	fright	angel	bright
might	acre	mighty	had	bad	waste	rad
mad	cut	major	put	taste	cute	sweet

Phonics for Older Students

Long /ā/

Silent 'e' a-e like take

Two Pencils and a Book

VCe

Vowel – Consonant – e

The silent e rule states that the e at the end of a syllable makes the vowel before it long or makes it "say its name."

The silent e is sometimes called magic e, silent e, or super e!

Some examples of this rule would be cake, take, and bake

The final e helps the vowel before the consonant say its name

cake

There can only be one consonant between the vowel and the e

Name: _____ Number: _____

Test Date 1: _____ Test Date 2: _____

Long A = /ā/
a-e
Teacher Page

Teacher Say: Put your finger on the first word. We are going to read down the column. Read each word. Begin.

Word	Correct	Word	Correct
cake		rate	
make		race	
came		wave	
take		save	
place		plane	
same		snake	
name		stage	
face		date	
page		whale	
late		flame	
case		sale	
shape		chase	
gave		pace	
state		escape	
space		became	

Name: _____ Number: _____

Test Date 1: _____ Test Date 2: _____

Long A = /ā/
a-e

Student Page

Word	Word
cake	rate
make	race
came	wave
take	save
place	plane
same	snake
name	stage
face	date
page	whale
late	flame
case	sale
shape	chase
gave	pace
state	escape
space	became

Long a – VCe – Magic e: a-e – List Three

Directions: Read each word three times. Shade in a triangle each time you read. △ △ △

cake	make	came	take	place
same	name	face	page	late
case	shape	gave	state	space

Directions: Underline the long a. Write each word four times.

cake				
make				
came				
take				
place				
same				
name				
face				
page				
late				
case				
shape				
gave				
state				
space				

Name: _____ Number: _____

Long a – VCe – Magic e: a-e

Directions: Read the sentences three times each. Shade in a triangle after each read. △ △ △

1. I baked a cake.
2. Emma will make a cake.
3. We came with a cake.
4. Take the cake to the table.
5. Juan won first place.
6. We have the same shirts.
7. His name is Bob.
8. Face the front of the room.
9. Turn to page six.
10. We went to be too late. Now, I'm tired.
11. I need a new case for my phone.
12. The shape is a circle.
13. He gave Emma a ring.
14. What state do you live in?
15. I need my space

Directions: Write four sentences using the long a words above.

1. _____

_____

2. _____

_____

3. _____

_____

Long a: VCe – Magic e - Three

Jake loved to bake. He baked two cakes a day. Today he was making a cake for a	18
contest.	19
"What cakes will you make?" Emma asked.	26
"I'll make the same as last year. It's too late to make a different cake," Jake said.	43
"I like the cake you made. It's the one in the heart shape, right?" Emma asked.	59
"Yes, it's the one in the heart shape. I have to make that cake," Jake said.	75
"Why?" Emma asked. "Why do you have to make that one?"	86
"My case is in the shape of a heart. My girl gave it to me. It's the same shape as the	107
cake. It makes it easy to carry my cake."	116
"Where do you have to go?" Emma asked.	125
"I'm going to another state. The cake needs its own space. That's why I use the	141
case."	142
"Do you think you'll win?" Emma asked.	149
"Hope so," he said. "Wanna taste?" Jake held out a spoon.	160

Words Read:	Words Read:	Words Read:
minus mistakes:	minus mistakes:	minus mistakes:
equals wpms:	equals wpms:	equals wpms:

1. Why is Jake baking? _____

2. What is the main idea of the reading? _____
_____
_____

3. Write two details that support the main idea. _____
_____
_____
_____

4. Write one sentence to finish the reading? _____
_____
_____

Name: _____ Number: _____

Long a – VCe – Magic e: a-e – List 4

Directions: Read each word three times. Shade in a triangle each time you read. △ △ △

rate	race	wave	save	plane
snake	stage	date	whale	flame
sale	chase	pace	escape	became

Directions: Underline the long a. Write each word four times.

rate				
snake				
sale				
race				
stage				
chase				
wave				
date				
pace				
save				
whale				
escape				
plane				
flame				
became				

Long a – VCe – Magic e: a-e

Directions: Read the sentences three times each. Shade in a triangle after each read. △ △ △

1. What did you rate the book?
2. Don't let the snake bit you.
3. I got these on sale.
4. She will sing on stage.
5. The dog will chase the cat.
6. Wave to the crowd.
7. What date is your trip?
8. They set a fast pace for the race.
9. Save your cards. We have a Bingo.
10. The whale jumped out of the water.
11. Will the snake escape?
12. The plane landed at the airport.
13. The flame jumped out of the fire.
14. What became of the cake?
15. He won the race.

Directions: Write four sentences using the long a words above.

1. _____

_____

2. _____

_____

3. _____

_____

Long a: VCe – Magic e – List 4

Jake put the snake back in its case. He'd chased it all over the island. It had	17
escaped. He didn't want it to escape again.	25
Jake and his friends were on vacation. He rescued the snake from the jaws of a	41
large bird. Jake watched the snake in its case.	50
"We're going to hit the waves," Marco said. "You coming?"	60
"Naw," said Jake. "I'll going to stay with the snake. I don't want it to escape again."	77
"What are you going to do with it? You can't get it on the plane," Marco said.	95
"I saved it. I can't just let it go," said Jake.	106
"You've missed two days of our vacation. You missed whale watching. You missed	119
the date with your old flame," Marco said.	127
"That wasn't the snake. That was me not going. I'm not going to chase someone	142
who dumped me. Stop trying to stage a date," Jake said.	153
"Hey Marco," Amy called from the water. "Pick up the pace. We're missing the	167
waves."	168
"Gotta go. Catch you later," Marco said. He headed for the waves.	180
"I'll be here with my snake," said Jake.	188

Words Read:	Words Read:	Words Read:
minus mistakes:	minus mistakes:	minus mistakes:
equals wpms:	equals wpms:	equals wpms:

1. What is the main idea of the reading? _____
_____
_____

2. Write two details that support the main idea. _____
_____
_____
_____

3. Write one or two sentences to expanding the reading? _____
_____
_____

Name: _____ Number: _____

Long a: VCe – Magic e Cloze Reading

Directions: Fill in the blanks with the correct long a word. Words may be used more than once.

Kate watched the flame. It gave off a red glow. She poked the fire. She looked at her

phone. It was getting late. She poked the fire again. Jake was late. He was never

_____. The race was over hours ago.

"Jake's taking his sweet time. He was supposed to pick us up at ten," Kate said.

"He's coming from the airport. Maybe his sister's _____. was late. What's her

_____. again?" Emily asked.

"Her name's Blake. At this rate, we'll never get home," Kate said. She poked the fire

again. The _____. glowed.

"He'll be here soon. Hey, you had a great race. You set the pace for the leaders. You won

first _____.," Emily said.

"The best part was the cake after the race," Kate said.

"Not your record-breaking _____.?" Emily asked.

"No, it was the cake. I came for the chocolate _____.," Kate laughed.

"Did you save any for Jake?" Emily asked.

"I was going to. I had a piece shaped like a heart. I ate it," Kate said. "Here he comes.

Blake _____. too."

"Sorry we're late. Blake's plane came late. How was the _____.?" Jake asked.

"Kate won," Emily said.

"The best part was the cake," Kate said. "I tried to _____. you some. It didn't

work. Hi Blake. Welcome to the state of Colorado."

Word Bank				
save	race	came	cake	pace
place	flame	name	plane	late

Two Pencils and a Book

Name: _____ Number: _____

Long a: VCe – Magic e Word Search

Directions: Find the long a words. The words can be up or down, left to right, or diagonal.

```
T  A  N  K  E  S  T  A  T  E  N  A  K  E  S  H  A  K
B  R  A  T  E  R  E  C  A  S  E  A  K  T  A  K  E  B
L  A  M  A  K  E  K  E  R  A  T  E  D  F  V  A  T  E
P  S  E  P  A  I  N  P  F  I  P  L  A  C  E  A  N  S
A  H  F  M  A  M  E  B  L  L  O  V  T  E  S  S  A  A
G  A  P  L  A  N  E  C  A  K  E  M  E  A  Y  N  T  M
E  K  L  Y  P  L  A  Y  M  P  A  S  T  E  W  A  V  E
A  E  A  C  O  R  A  C  E  R  N  A  B  L  E  K  B  A
S  C  C  O  N  B  A  B  Y  W  H  A  L  E  P  E  A  P
P  E  E  R  C  A  M  E  L  A  D  S  Y  S  T  A  T  A
I  B  E  C  A  M  E  O  N  C  H  A  S  E  R  L  A  C
S  H  A  P  E  D  G  A  V  E  O  L  I  S  T  A  G  E
O  F  A  M  O  U  S  P  A  C  E  E  S  M  A  T  O  R
T  A  E  S  C  A  P  E  S  T  E  M  F  A  C  E  A  P
```

Word Bank

cake	rate	take	save	name	stage	late	flame
make	race	place	plane	face	date	case	sale
came	wave	same	snake	page	whale	shape	chase
	gave	pace	escape	state	space	became	

Name: _____ Number: _____

Word Maze Long A Words

Directions: Follow the LONG A words to the END. You may move up and down or left and right.

START	rain	main	play	day	may	pay
acorn	bay	faithful	way	ray	say	clay
able	pray	rainy	display	sleep	agree	guarantee
bacon	aim	maintain	today	display	array	today
potato	sleep	delay	relay	holiday	essay	betrayal
crazy	basic	Asia	baby	employee	steep	queen
waiting	plainly	domain	paper	pray	saying	display
breeze	payable	may	lady	read	bread	breed
feed	labor	favor	nation	zookeeper	volunteer	employee
degree	basis	guarantee	draining	exclaim	peace	peaceful
feature	alien	teenager	clean	frail	beneath	decrease
reason	radio	season	engineer	raisin	see	tree
famous	station	season	reason	attain	teach	creature
data	queen	beaver	degree	paint	contain	waitress
acre	freeze	overseen	cheer	beneath	beach	rain
angel	waste	major	taste	maple	paste	END

Name: _____ Number: _____

Circle the Long A Words

Directions: Circle the Long A words.

acorn	bread	breed	the	mason	time	Asia
able	when	fatal	where	were	hog	native
dog	baby	cat	paste	crazy	dog	queen
paper	tree	out	round	ground	mouth	doubt
about	loud	able	loudmouth	pound	nation	mount
account	astound	doubt	maple	doubtful	aloud	bouncy
crazy	amount	recount	thousand	grew	favor	shout
grew	crew	chew	flew	drew	stew	knew
famous	dew	view	blew	bacon	brew	new
threw	basic	news	labor	cashew	jewelry	Preview
nephew	review	basis	preview	interview	curfew	potato
sigh	high	thigh	light	alien	something	green
red	station	blue	flight	night	might	right
data	sight	tight	radio	fright	angel	bright
might	acre	mighty	had	bad	waste	rad
mad	cut	major	put	taste	cute	sweet

Set One Answers

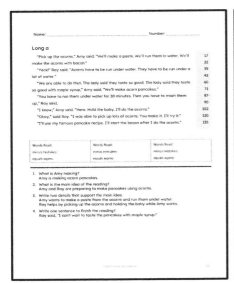

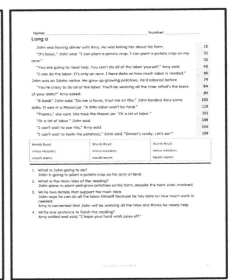

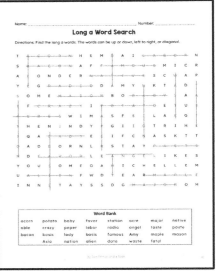

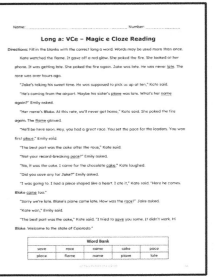

Set One Answers

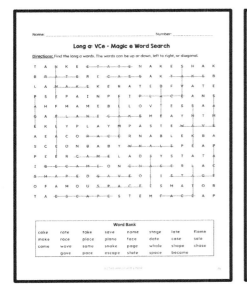

Long a: VCe - Magic e Word Search

Directions: Find the long a words. The words can be up or down, left to right, or diagonal.

Word Bank

cake	rate	take	save	name	stage	late	flame
make	race	place	plane	face	date	case	sale
came	wave	same	snake	page	whale	shape	chase
	gave	pace	escape	state	space	became	

Word Maze

Directions: Follow the LONG A words to the END. You may move up and down or left and right.

START	rain	main	play	day	may	pay
acorn	bay	faithful	way	ray	say	clay
able	pray	rainy	display	sleep	agree	guarantee
bacon	aim	maintain	today	display	array	today
potato	sleep	delay	relay	holiday	essay	betrayal
crazy	basic	Asia	baby	employee	sleep	queen
waiting	plainly	domain	paper	pray	saying	display
breeze	payable	may	lady	read	bread	breed
feed	labor	favor	nation	zookeeper	volunteer	employee
degree	basis	guarantee	draining	exclaim	peace	peaceful
feature	alien	teenager	clean	frail	beneath	decrease
reason	radio	season	engineer	raisin	see	tree
famous	station	season	reason	attain	teach	creature
data	queen	beaver	degree	paint	contain	waitress
acre	freeze	overseen	cheer	beneath	beach	rain
angel	waste	major	taste	maple	paste	END

Circle the Long A Words

Directions: Circle the Long A words.

acorn	bread	breed	the	mason	time	Asia
able	when	fatal	where	were	hog	native
dog	baby	cat	paste	crazy	dog	queen
paper	tree	out	round	ground	mouth	doubt
about	loud	able	loudmouth	pound	nation	mount
account	astound	doubt	maple	doubtful	aloud	bouncy
crazy	amount	recount	thousand	grew	favor	shout
grew	crew	chew	flew	drew	stew	knew
famous	dew	view	blew	bacon	brew	new
threw	basic	news	labor	cashew	jewelry	Preview
nephew	review	basis	preview	interview	curfew	potato
sigh	high	thigh	light	alien	something	green
red	station	blue	flight	night	might	right
data	sight	tight	radio	fright	angel	bright
might	acre	mighty	had	bad	waste	rad
mod	cut	major	put	taste	cute	sweet

Two Pencils and a Book

Phonics for Older Students

Long /ā/

Vowel Team ai

Vowel Team 'ai'

VV

"ai" is a vowel team
"ai" says a
long / a /

a-i

r a i n

Multi-Syllable
"ai" Vowel Team Fluency Passages

Waiting for the Train   Lexile Level 200L
The Sailboat   Lexile Level 200L
The First Date   Lexile Level 225L
The Big Win   Lexile Level 250L
The Domain Name   Lexile Level 275L

Teaching Presentation at
Guided Worksheet presentation available at:
https://docs.google.com/presentation/d/1Vcma6UjeuI8d4gXqzgSlUNeROfb7MtX_fj3GsFyF9VU/edit?usp=sharing

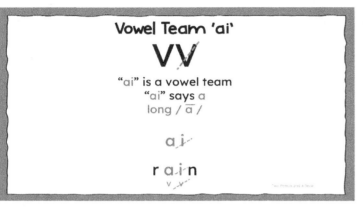

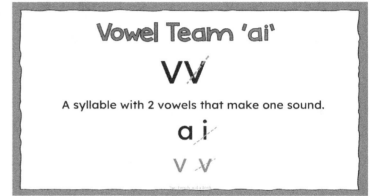

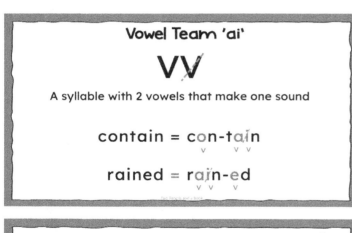

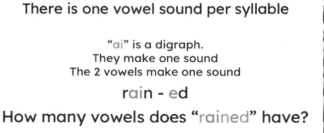

Name: _____ Number: _____

Test Date 1: _____ Test Date 2: _____

"ai" Vowel Team
Teacher Page

Teacher Say: Put your finger on the first word. We are going to read down the column. Read each word. Begin.

Word	Correct	Word	Correct	Word	Correct
rain		explain		aim	
main		maintain		claim	
pain		contain		braid	
gain		attain		drain	
train		retain		nailed	
stain		faithful		detail	
paint		plainly		gained	
fail		waiting		domain	
wait		regain		prepaid	
snail		complaint		unpaid	
mail		afraid		raisin	
sail		rainy		frail	
refrain		draining		proclaim	
remain		exclaim		faithful	
complain		unpaid		waitress	

Name: _____ Number: _____

Test Date 1: _____ Test Date 2: _____

"ai" Vowel Team
"ai" says "ay" – Long /a/
Student Page

Word	Word	Word
rain	explain	aim
main	maintain	claim
pain	contain	braid
gain	attain	drain
train	retain	nailed
stain	faithful	detail
paint	plainly	gained
fail	waiting	domain
wait	regain	prepaid
snail	complaint	unpaid
mail	afraid	raisin
sail	rainy	frail
refrain	draining	proclaim
remain	exclaim	faithful
complain	unpaid	waitress

Paste small rectangle into notebook to make a flap.

Vowel Team "ai" Digraph

Paste into notebook

'ai" Digraph

A digraph is **two letters that make one sound.**

"ai" makes the long /a/ sound.

Word Pocket

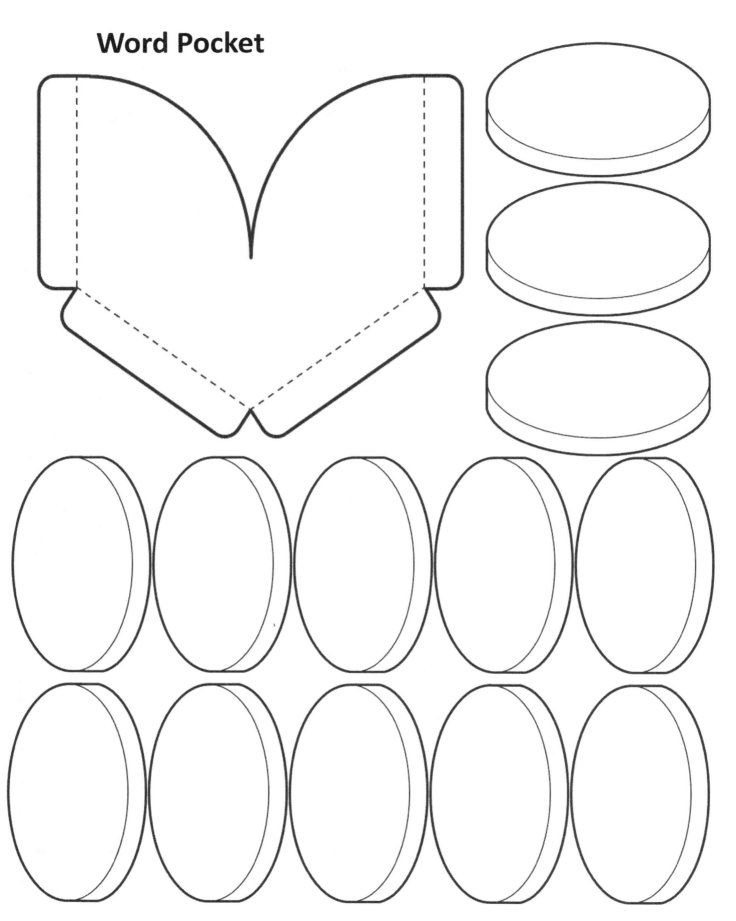

Put one word on each of coins. Cut out. Paste the pocket to your notebook and fill the pocket with coins.

Two Pencils and a Book

Put one word on each of coins. Cut out. Paste the pocket to your notebook and fill the pocket with coins.

Two Pencils and a Book

Long a – Vowel Team 'ai'

Directions: Read each word three times. Shade in a triangle each time you read.

rain	gain	paint	snail	claim
main	train	fail	mail	braid
pain	stain	wait	aim	drain

Directions: Underline the long a. Write each word four times.

rain				
main				
pain				
gain				
train				
stain				
paint				
fail				
wait				
snail				
mail				
aim				
claim				
braid				
drain				

Long a – Vowel Team 'ai'

Directions: Read the sentences three times each. Shade in a triangle after each read. △ △ △

1. They stopped the game because of the rain.
2. The main part of the game was missing.
3. The fall caused his leg great pain.
4. It looks like the runner will gain the lead.
5. We took the train to the city.
6. That juice will stain your shirt.
7. The red paint looked great on the door.
8. I don't want to fail the test.
9. The snail left a trail on the flower.
10. The postcard came in the mail.
11. His aim with the baseball was great.
12. File a claim for the lost phone.
13. She had a braid in her hair.
14. Wait for the new song to drop.
15. The drain was plugged with hair.

Directions: Write four sentences using the long a words from List One.

1. _____

_____

2. _____

_____

3. _____

_____

Long a – Vowel Team 'ai ' – Passage 5

Emma checked her mail. She checked her mail on the way to the train. She was	17
going to a photo contest. Her photo was of a snail. The snail had left a trail. The trail	22
glowed in the photo.	39
"What's your aim for the contest?" John asked.	42
"My aim is to claim first prize," Emma said. "If I claim first prize, I'll get more	60
followers."	71
"More followers can be a pain," John said.	87
"You say that because you don't need more followers. But I do, and it's a pain I	90
want. My account when down the drain. My account went down the drain when I was	102
stuck in the rain."	120
"You spent two weeks stuck in the rain. What did you think would happen?" John	135

asked.

"I thought the roads would not wash away," Emma said. "Come on the train's here. Let's go see if I can claim a prize."

Words Read:	Words Read:	Words Read:
minus mistakes:	minus mistakes:	minus mistakes:
equals wpms:	equals wpms:	equals wpms:

1. What is the main idea of the reading? _____
_____
_____

2. Write two details that support the main idea. _____
_____
_____
_____

3. Write one sentence to finish the reading? _____
_____
_____

Sentence Fluency: "ai"

We took the train.	04
We took the train in the rain.	11
It was raining when we took the train.	19
We had to wait for the train.	26
We had to wait for the main train.	34
We had to wait for the train in the rain.	44
We had to wait for the main train in the rain.	55
The rain stained his shoes.	60
The rain plainly stained his shoes.	66
The mail was on the train.	72
The train contained the mail.	77
The train stopped to drop off the mail.	85
It was a pain to wait in the rain.	94
It was a pain to wait in the rain for the train.	106
Our train tickets were unpaid.	111
We had to pay for our tickets.	118
We had to pay for our tickets before we could get on the train.	132
We got on the train.	137
The train had to regain speed.	143
We can't complain.	146
We can't complain because the train ride was great.	155

Words Read: _____	Words Read: _____	Words Read: _____
minus mistakes: _____	minus mistakes: _____	minus mistakes: _____
equals wpms: _____	equals wpms: _____	equals wpms: _____

Fluency: "ai" – 200L – Waiting for the Train – Passage 6

"I'm getting wet!" Mateo exclaimed.	05
"I'm getting soaking wet!" Ana exclaimed while waiting in the rain. They	17
were waiting in the rain for the train.	25
"The rain will stain my shoes," Mateo said.	33
"No, the rain won't stain. Your shoes will dry," Ava said.	44
"I hope so," Mateo said. "I hope we don't have to wait long."	57
"I'm afraid the train is already late," Ava said.	66
"I can't be late for school," Mateo said. "The art show is first period. I have	82
to get my painting there."	87
"There's not much we can do. We have to wait for the train. We can't just	103
make it appear."	106
"Why is the main train always late?" Mateo said. "You'd think they'd figure	119
that out."	121
"You'd think," Ana said. "Where's your painting? It's not getting rained on,	133
is it?"	135
"No, it's here," Mateo said. He held up a plastic case. "Look!" He pointed	149
down the rail. "The train's coming."	155
"Finally," Ana said. "Let's get that painting to school."	164

Words Read: _____	Words Read: _____	Words Read: _____
minus mistakes: _____	minus mistakes: _____	minus mistakes: _____
equals wpms: _____	equals wpms: _____	equals wpms: _____

Fluency Comprehension: "ai" Waiting for the Train

Directions: Please select the best response.

1. What does Mateo say is happening first period?

   a. a test

   b. a field trip

   c. he gets to paint

   d. an art show

2. What does Mateo say is always late?

   a. the train is always late

   b. the main train is always late

   c. they are always late getting to school

   d. Mrs. Green is always late

3. Read the first paragraph. What is the best definition for the word <u>exclaimed</u>?

   a. said

   b. whispered

   c. called out

   d. screamed

5. What is the reading mostly about?

   a. a train

   b. waiting for the train in the rain

   c. an art show

   d. two people in the rain

The vowels "ai" makes the long /a/ sound in words like rain, pain, wait, aim.

Write each word three times, then underline the "ai" vowel team in the words below.

Write rain three times. Underline the vowel team.

_____   _____   _____

Write painting three times. Underline the vowel team.

_____   _____   _____

Write wait three times. Underline the vowel team.

_____   _____   _____

Write stain three times. Underline the vowel team.

_____   _____   _____

Name: _____ Number: _____

"ai" Waiting for the Train – Cloze Reading

Directions: Fill in the blanks with the correct "ai" word. Words may be used more than once.

"I'm getting wet!" Mateo exclaimed.

"I'm getting soaking wet!" Ana _____ while waiting in the rain. They were waiting in the _____ for the train.

"The rain will _____ my shoes," Mateo said.

"No, the rain won't stain. Your shoes will dry," Ava said.

"I hope so," Mateo said. "I hope we don't have to _____ long."

"I'm afraid the train is already late," Ava said.

"I can't be late for school," Mateo said. "The art show is first period. I have to get my painting there."

"There's not much we can do. We have to wait for the _____. We can't just make it appear."

"Why is the main _____ always late?" Mateo said. "You'd think they'd figure that out."

"You'd think," Ana said. "Where's your _____? It's not getting rained on, is it?"

"No, it's here," Mateo said. He held up a plastic case. "Look!" He pointed down the rail. "The _____ is coming."

"Finally," Ana said. "Let's get that painting to school."

Word Bank			
train	exclaimed	wait	stain
rain	train	painting	train

Fluency: "ai" – 200L – The Sailboat – Passage 7

Joe and Kyle like to sail. They sail every weekend. This weekend they were	14
sailing to Montauk.	17
There was a problem. They got to the boat. They found water. They found	31
water at the bottom of the sailboat.	38
"Must have been the rain," Joe said. "It has been raining hard."	50
"Or a hole," Kyle proclaimed.	55
"Pull the drain and see what happens," Joe said.	64
"I'll tell you what happens. The boat will fill with water. The boat will fill	79
with water if you pull the drain."	86
"Then why's there a drain?" Joe asked.	93
"For when the boat's on land. The drain can only be pulled on land."	107
They got the boat out of the water. They pulled the drain. The boat was	122
draining. They looked over the boat. There were no holes. A little paint was	136
chipped. But there were no holes.	142
"I'm not surprised. We maintain our boat well," Kyle said.	152
"Let's get it back in the water. I'm ready for a sail. Aim for Montauk," Joe	168
said.	170
"It's too late. Looking for the hole took to long. I have to be back for	186
work," Kyle said.	189
"I don't mean to complain," Joe said.	196
"But you will complain. What?" Kyle asked.	203
"You never used to work on Saturday. Now, it's all the time," Joe	216
complained.	217
"This is the last. The rain held us up. You sail today. We'll sail next	132
Saturday."	133
"Perfect. Don't work too hard. I'm off," Joe proclaimed.	142

Words Read: _____	Words Read: _____	Words Read: _____
minus mistakes: _____	minus mistakes: _____	minus mistakes: _____
equals wpms: _____	equals wpms: _____	equals wpms: _____

Fluency Comprehension: "ai" The Sailboat

Directions: Please select the best response.

1. What held up the sailing?
   a. the drain
   b. the rain
   c. the boat had a hole
   d. the boat was filled with water

2. Why couldn't Kyle sail?
   a. he had to work on the boat
   b. he had to work at his job
   c. they had to drain the boat
   d. the boat was filled with water

3. Re-read the sentence: "There was a <u>problem</u>." What does the word <u>problem</u> mean?
   a. something that is a worry and has to be fixed
   b. something that is messed up
   c. something that is odd
   d. something that is filled with water

4. What is the reading mostly about?
   a. sailing to Montauk
   b. a rain that filled a sailboat with water
   c. two friends talking and draining a sailboat
   d. working instead of sailing

The vowels "ai" makes the long /a/ sound in words like rain, pain, wait, aim.

Write each word three times, then underline the "ai" vowel team in the words below.

Write proclaim three times. Underline the vowel team.
_____ _____ _____

Write explain three times. Underline the vowel team.
_____ _____ _____

Write drain three times. Underline the vowel team.
_____ _____ _____

Write regain three times. Underline the vowel team.
_____ _____ _____

"ai" The Sailboat – Cloze Reading

Directions: Fill in the blanks with the correct "ai" word. Words may be used more than once.

Joe and Kyle like to sail. They sail every weekend. This weekend they were

_____ to Montauk.

There was a problem. They got to the boat. They found water. They found water at

the bottom of the the sailboat.

"Must have been the rain," Joe said. "It has been _____ pretty hard."

"Or a hole," Kyle proclaimed.

"Pull the _____ and see what happens," Joe said.

"I'll tell you what happens. The boat will fill with water. The boat will fill with water if

you pull the _____."

"Then why's there a _____?" Joe asked.

"For when the boat's on land. The drain can only be pulled on land."

They got the boat out of the water. They pulled the drain. The boat was

_____. They looked over the boat. There were no holes. A little paint was

chipped. But there were no holes.

"I'm not surprised. We _____ our boat well," Kyle said.

"Let's get it back in the water. I'm ready for a sail. Aim for Montauk," Joe said.

"_____ for Montauk and let's go."

"It's too late. Looking for the hole took to long. I have to be back for work," Kyle said.

Word Bank			
sailing	aim	draining	drain
drain	raining	maintain	drain

Fluency: "ai" – 225L – The First Date – Passage 8

AJ and Maria were on a date. It was their first date. AJ tried to make	16
everything great. And it started out fine. They went to a movie. They both	30
loved it. Then they went to dinner. That's where things fell apart.	42
"I'm filing a complaint," Maria said.	48
"Dinner was pretty bad," AJ said.	54
"Pretty bad!? It was the worst," Maria proclaimed.	62
"Well, not the worst…"	66
"And the waitress!?" Maria exclaimed.	71
"The one with the braids in her hair?"	79
"Yes, the one with the braids. I asked for no raisins. I wanted no raisins on	95
my salad," Maria explained. "I hate raisins."	102
"I know. I was there," AJ said. "But you didn't have to throw them."	116
"My aim was perfect."	120
"Remind me to never sit near the kitchen with you," AJ said.	132
"I hit the drain with all but one," Maria said.	142
"You don't throw raisins in public," AJ said.	150
"The sink was right there. I had to aim for the drain. She asked for it. I	167
asked for no raisins."	171
AJ shook his head. "Filing a complaint, I get. Throwing raisins. No so	184
much."	185
"What can I say?" Maria said.	191
"That you had a good time."	197
"I did! I had a great time!" Maria said.	206
"Next time we skip dinner," AJ said. "Deal?"	214
"Deal?" Maria said.	217

Words Read: _____	Words Read: _____	Words Read: _____
minus mistakes: _____	minus mistakes: _____	minus mistakes: _____
equals wpms: _____	equals wpms: _____	equals wpms: _____

Fluency Comprehension: "ai" The First Date

Directions: Please select the best response.

1. What did Maria do that AJ questioned?
   a. went to dinner with him
   b. wore braids
   c. ate a salad
   d. threw raisins

2. What is the theme or message in the reading?
   a. AJ and Maria have a great first date.
   b. AJ and Maria have a talk about a waitress with braids.
   c. Maria throws raisins in a restaurant.
   d. AJ and Maria decide to go out again.

3. Read first paragraph. What is the best definition for the word <u>complaint</u>?
   a. protest
   b. praise
   c. grumble
   d. honor

4. In the reading, what is the best definition for the word <u>proclaimed</u>?
   a. said
   b. declared
   c. whispered
   d. hid

Directions: Say the word in your head as you color each word. Underline the "ai" vowel team.

complaint, WAITRESS, RAISINS, proclaimed, drain, AIM, braids, DRAIN, complaint, WAITRESS, RAISINS, proclaimed, drain, AIM, braids, DRAIN

Name: _____ Number: _____

"ai" The First Date – Cloze Reading

Directions: Fill in the blanks with the correct "ai" word. Words may be used more than once.

AJ and Maria were on a date. It was their first date. AJ tried to make everything

great. And it started out fine. They went to a movie. They both loved it. Then they went

to dinner. That's where things fell apart.

"I'm filing a _____," Maria said.

"Dinner was pretty bad," AJ said.

"Pretty bad!? It was the worst," Maria _____.

"Well, not the worst…"

"And the _____?" Maria exclaimed.

"The one with the braids in her hair?"

"Yes, the one with the _____. I asked for no raisins. I wanted no

_____ on my salad," Maria explained. "I hate raisins."

"I know. I was there," AJ said. "But you didn't have to throw them."

"My _____ was perfect."

"Remind me to never sit near the kitchen with you," AJ said.

"I hit the _____ with all but one," Maria said.

"You don't throw raisins in public," AJ said.

"The sink was right there. I had to aim for the drain. She asked for it. I asked for no

_____."

Word Bank			
drain	raisins	braids	aim
braids	waitress	proclaimed	complaint

Fluency: "ai" – 250L – The Big Win – Passage 9

"Dig! Dig for the ball!" Coach exclaimed. "No pain, no gain! Dig!"	05
Mila flew towards the ball. She got under it just it time.	17
"My ball!" Emma exclaimed.	25
"Set it," Coach said.	33
Emma set the ball. Ava spiked it. Over the net it went. Ava hit her mark	44
without fail.	57
"Nailed it!" Emma said. "Set and match!"	66
"We remain undefeated!" Ava said.	82
"Great job team!" Coach said.	87
The team gathered around Coach Smith.	103
"I had faith you would win. You played all out! Now, go claim your trophy."	106
"Take that Tigers!" Emma yelled.	119
"Emma," Coach said. "Refrain from bragging. Good sportsmanship and	121
all."	133
"Sorry," Emma said. "I'm just so excited. I can barely contain myself."	135
Coach smiled. "No worries. Just be mindful of the other team."	149
"Got it Coach," Emma said. "I'll remain calm. But yay! We won!" Emma said	155
softly. Then, she ran off to join the team.	164

Words Read: _____	Words Read: _____	Words Read: _____
minus mistakes: _____	minus mistakes: _____	minus mistakes: _____
equals wpms: _____	equals wpms: _____	equals wpms: _____

Fluency Comprehension: "ai" The Big Win

Directions: Please select the best response.

1. What was the last thing Emma did?
   a. Exclaim "We won!"
   b. Join the team.
   c. Set the ball.
   d. Spike the ball.

2. What is the theme or message in the reading?
   a. winning and teamwork
   b. friendship and winning
   c. teamwork and friendship
   d. sportsmanship and teamwork

3. Read the first paragraph. What is the best definition for the word underlined exclaimed?
   a. called out
   b. whispered
   c. cried
   d. said

4. In the reading, what is the best definition for the word underlined refrain?
   a. keep going
   b. hold back or stop
   c. move forward
   d. chorus of a song

Directions: Say the word in your head as you color each word. Underline the "ai" vowel team.

faith, NAILED, pain, GAIN,

refrain, REMAIN, contain,

faith, NAILED, pain, GAIN,

refrain, REMAIN, contain

faith, NAILED, pain, GAIN,

refrain, REMAIN, contain

Name: _____   Number: _____

"ai" The Big Win – Cloze Reading

Directions: Fill in the blanks with the correct "ai" word. Words may be used more than once.

"Dig! Dig for the ball!" Coach exclaimed. "No pain, no _____! Dig!"

Mila flew towards the ball. She got under it just it time.

"My ball!" Emma _____.

"Set it," Coach said.

Emma set the ball. Ava spiked it. Over the net it went. Ava hit her mark without

_____.

"Nailed it!" Emma said. "Set and match!"

"We _____ undefeated!" Ava said.

"Great job team!" Coach said.

The team gathered around Coach Smith.

"I had _____ you would win. You played all out! Now, go claim your trophy."

"Take that Tigers!" Emma yelled.

"Emma," Coach said. "_____ from bragging. Good sportsmanship and all."

"Sorry," Emma said. "I'm just so excited. I can barely _____ myself."

Coach smiled. "No worries. Just be mindful of the other team."

"Got it Coach," Emma said. "I'll _____ calm. But yay! We won!" Emma said

softly. Then, she ran off to join the team.

Word Bank			
exclaimed	faith	refrain	contain
remain	gain	remain	fail

Fluency: "ai" – 275L – The Domain Name Passage 10

Danny ran to the door. He grabbed the mail.	09
"Let me see," Jake said. Jake is Danny's brother. "I wanted to look first."	23
"You move like a snail."	28
"Is it there? Did we regain the domain?" Jake asked.	38
"I don't know," Danny said.	43
"Well, look through the mail," Jake said.	50
They were talking about their domain name. They owned a website. Then,	62
they lost the name. Now, they were trying to get it back.	74
"Here it is. A balance remains, but we got it back."	85
"I thought we prepaid for the website? I thought we prepaid the domain?"	98
"We prepaid most of it," Danny said. "We paid enough. It's ours again."	111
There it was. It was written plainly on the paper. They did it. They got their	127
domain name back.	130
"Yep, plain as day. Now, we can start branding our name," Jake said.	143
They'd been waiting a long time for this.	151
"Let's not waste another minute. Let's go upload our logo," Danny said.	163
"Let's upload our whole website," Jake said. "Then we'll put it out on social	177
media."	178
Their website was up within an hour. Their business was booming within a	191
week.	192

Words Read: _____	Words Read: _____	Words Read: _____
minus mistakes: _____	minus mistakes: _____	minus mistakes: _____
equals wpms: _____	equals wpms: _____	equals wpms: _____

Fluency Comprehension: "ai" The Domain Name

Directions: Please select the best response.

1. What did Danny and Jake regain?
   a. only their website
   b. their domain name
   c. their prepaid phone
   d. their business

2. What did Danny and Jake upload?
   a. their domain name and their website
   b. their brand
   c. their domain name
   d. their website

3. Re-read the sentence: "It was written <u>plainly</u> on paper." What does the word <u>plainly</u> mean?
   a. clearly
   b. directly
   c. barely
   d. bluntly

4. What is the reading mostly about?
   a. a domain name
   b. brothers who get their website back
   c. brothers who get their domain name back
   d. none of the above

The vowels "ai" makes the long /a/ sound in words like rain, pain, wait, aim.

Write each word three times, then underline the "ai" vowel team in the words below.

Write the word domain three times. Underline the vowel team.

_____   _____   _____

Write plainly three times. Underline the vowel team.

_____   _____   _____

Write wait three times. Underline the vowel team.

_____   _____   _____

Write regain three times. Underline the vowel team.

_____   _____   _____

"ai" The Domain Name – Cloze Reading

Directions: Fill in the blanks with the correct "ai" word. Words may be used more than once.

Danny ran to the door. He grabbed the mail.

"Let me see," Jake said. Jake was his brother. "I wanted to look first."

"You move like a snail. I got here first. I'll open the _____."

"Is it there? Did we _____ the domain?" Jake asked.

"I don't know," Danny said.

"Well, look through the _____," Jake said.

They were talking about their _____ name. They owned a website. Then, they

lost the name. Now, they were trying to get it back.

"Here it is. A balance remains, but we got it back."

"I thought we prepaid for the website? I thought we _____ the domain?"

"We prepaid most of it," Danny said. "We paid enough. It's ours again."

There it was. It was written _____ on the paper. They did it. They got their

domain name back.

"Yep, plain as day. Now, we can start branding our name," Jake said.

They'd been waiting a long time for this. Now they had it. They had their

_____ name back.

"Let's not waste another minute. Let's go upload our logo," Danny said.

"Let's upload our whole website," Jake said. "Then we'll put it out on social media."

Their website was up within an hour. Their business was booming within a week.

Word Bank			
regain	mail	domain	prepaid
domain	domain	plainly	mail

Name: _____ Number: _____

Vowel Team "ai" Word Search

Directions: Find the "ai" words. The words can be up or down, left to right, or diagonal.

```
T  R  A  I  N  H  E  S  A  I  L  O  B  R  A  I  D  S
L  E  L  E  P  H  A  N  B  S  T  A  I  N  A  I  L  T
A  M  A  I  N  T  A  I  N  O  H  T  E  M  E  L  R  A
I  A  T  U  P  L  A  I  N  L  Y  U  D  O  A  P  E  I
R  I  S  E  G  O  H  L  I  O  P  I  E  D  O  I  P  N
A  N  D  X  E  P  E  A  C  K  L  K  T  A  L  E  L  P
I  S  N  C  I  P  R  A  I  N  Y  N  A  N  Y  T  H  T
N  P  O  L  P  L  C  O  I  L  C  W  I  K  J  A  T  W
Y  A  N  A  I  L  P  T  C  O  M  I  L  T  I  T  I  A
D  R  A  I  N  I  N  G  D  L  O  V  E  S  N  T  A  I
M  A  N  M  A  D  E  N  A  E  A  V  E  L  T  A  R  T
T  H  E  R  A  F  R  A  I  L  E  I  P  T  Y  I  N  I
E  N  T  R  A  I  N  G  L  A  D  O  M  A  I  N  E  N
G  A  I  N  E  D  N  D  S  L  A  I  T  E  L  D  B  G
```

Word Bank

detail	waiting	rain	remain	maintain	proclaim	stain	exclaim
waiting	gained	rainy	domain	attain	braids	draining	main
sail	fail	plainly	train	stain	rainy	faithful	frail

Name: _____ Number: _____

'ai' Vowel Team

Across
1. A hairstyle. Interwoven strands of hair.
4. A fall of water from the sky.
5. To call out.
8. To keep up or carry on; continue.
9. To tell all about something.

Down
2. A part of something d _ _ t _ _ l.
3. To protest against something or someone.
4. To stain in one place.
6. In a plain manner.
7. To discolor, get dirty, or spot.

Vowel Team 'ai' Word Maze

Directions: Follow the "ai" words to the END. You may move up and down or left and right.

START	rain	main	play	day	may	pay
stay	bay	faithful	way	ray	say	clay
spray	pray	rainy	display	sleep	agree	guarantee
claim	aim	maintain	today	display	array	today
gain	sleep	delay	relay	holiday	essay	betrayal
pain	deep	haystack	way	employee	steep	queen
waiting	plainly	domain	afraid	pray	saying	display
breeze	payable	may	prepaid	read	bread	breed
feed	horse	house	sail	zookeeper	volunteer	employee
degree	spray	guarantee	draining	exclaim	peace	peaceful
feature	trainee	teenager	clean	frail	beneath	decrease
reason	zookeeper	season	engineer	raisin	see	tree
feel	sleepover	season	reason	attain	teach	creature
theater	queen	beaver	degree	paint	contain	waitress
beaver	freeze	overseen	cheer	beneath	beach	rain
beat	meat	read	feed	speak	weave	END

RAIN, RAIN, RAIN,

sustain, sustain, sustain,

MAIL, MAIL MAIL

complain, complain, complain,

GAIN, GAIN, GAIN

detail, detail, detail

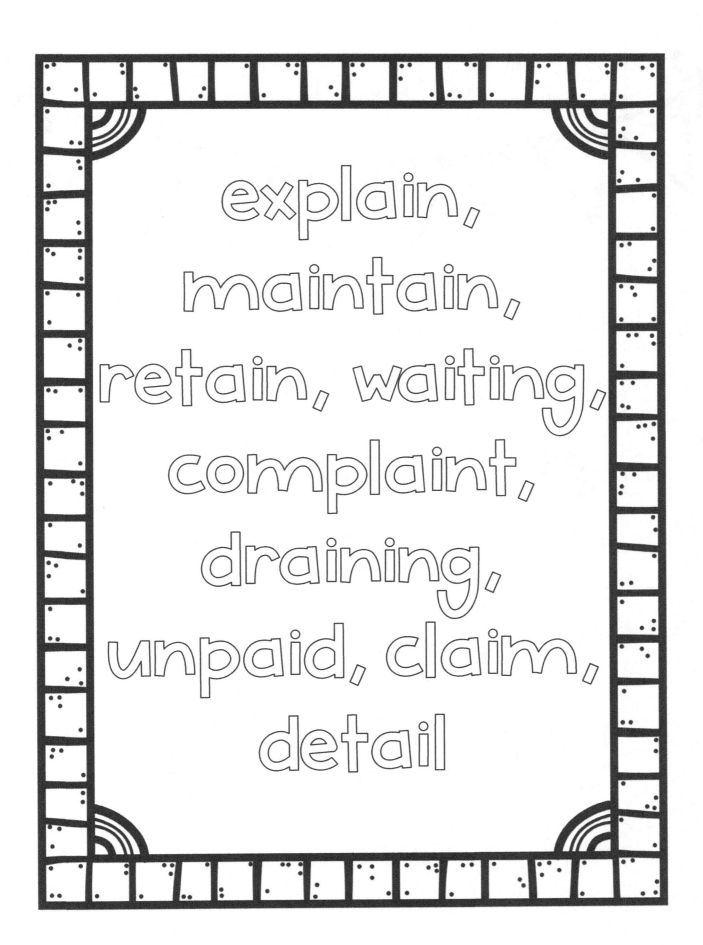

explain, maintain, retain, waiting, complaint, draining, unpaid, claim, detail

"ai" Vowel Team

explain, maintain, retain, waiting, complaint, draining, unpaid, claim, detail

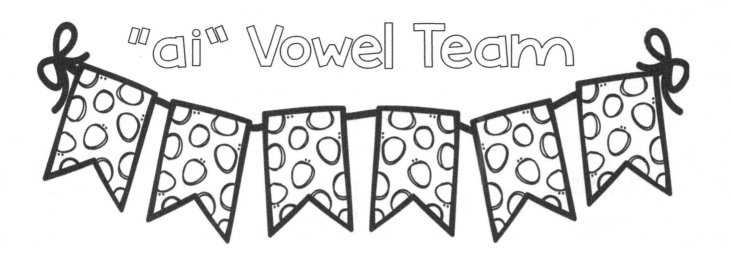

"ai" Vowel Team

proclaim, sail, attain, braid, retain, aim, detail, mail, proclaim, nail, waitress

"ai" Vowel Team
"ai" says "ay" – Long /a/
Guided Worksheet

1. rain	16. explain
2. main	17. maintain
3. pain	18. contain
4. gain	19. attain
5. train	20. retain
6. waitress	21. faithful
7. detail	22. plainly
8. gained	23. waiting
9. domain	24. regain
10. prepaid	25. complaint
11. unpaid	26. afraid
12. raisin	27. rainy
13. refrain	28. draining
14. remain	29. exclaim
15. complain	30. unpaid

Name: _____ Number: _____

Test Date 1: _____ Test Date 2: _____

"ai" Vowel Team
Final "ai" Worksheet

Directions. Divide each word into syllables and then underline the "ai" vowel team.

Example: sus/t<u>ai</u>n		
rain	explain	aim
main	maintain	claim
pain	contain	braid
gain	attain	drain
train	retain	nailed
stain	faithful	detail
paint	plainly	gained
fail	waiting	domain
wait	regain	prepaid
snail	complaint	unpaid
mail	afraid	raisin
sail	rainy	frail
refrain	draining	proclaim
remain	exclaim	faithful
complain	unpaid	waitress

Fluency Comprehension: "ai" Waiting for the Train

Directions: Please select the best response.

1. What does Mateo say is happening first period?
   a. a test
   b. a field trip
   c. he gets to paint
   d. an art show

2. What does Mateo say is always late?
   a. the train is always late
   b. the main train is always late
   c. they are always late getting to school
   d. Mrs. Green is always late

3. Read first paragraph. What is the best definition for the word exclaimed?
   a. said
   b. whispered
   c. called out
   d. screamed

5. What is the reading mostly about?
   a. a train
   b. waiting for the train in the rain
   c. an art show
   d. two people in the rain

The vowels "ai" makes the long /a/ sound in words like rain, pain, wait, aim.

Underline the "ai" vowel team in the words below

Write rain three times. Underline the vowel team.

Write painting three times. Underline the vowel team.

Write wait three times. Underline the vowel team.

Write stain three times. Underline the vowel team.

"ai" Waiting for the Train – Cloze Reading

Directions: Fill in the blanks with the correct "ai" word. Words may be used more than once.

"I'm getting wet!" Mateo exclaimed.

"I'm getting soaking wet!" Ana _____ exclaimed while waiting in the rain. They were waiting in the _____ rain for the train.

"The rain will _____ stain my shoes," Mateo said.

"No, the rain won't stain. Your shoes will dry," Ava said.

"I hope so," Mateo said. "I hope we don't have to _____ wait long."

"I'm afraid the train is already late," Ava said.

"I can't be late for school," Mateo said. "The art show is first period. I have to get my painting there."

"There's not much we can do. We have to wait for the _____ train. We can't just make it appear."

"Why is the main _____ train always late?" Mateo said. "You'd think they'd figure that out."

"You'd think," Ana said. "Where's your _____ painting? It's not getting ruined on, is it?"

"No, it's here," Mateo said. He held up a plastic case. "Look!" He pointed down the rail. "The _____ is coming."

"Finally," Ana said. "Let's get that painting to school."

Word Bank			
train	exclaimed	wait	stain
rain	train	painting	train

Fluency Comprehension: "ai" The Domain Name

Directions: Please select the best response.

1. What held up the sailing?
   a. the drain
   b. the rain
   c. the boat had a hole
   d. the boat was filled with water

2. Why couldn't Kyle sail?
   a. he had to work on the boat
   b. he had to work at his job
   c. they had to drain the boat
   d. the boat was filled with water

3. Re-read the sentence: "There was a problem." What does the word problem mean?
   a. something that is a worry and has to be fixed
   b. something that is messed up
   c. something that is odd
   d. something that is filled with water

4. What is the reading mostly about?
   a. sailing to Montauk
   b. a rain that filled a sailboat with water
   c. two friends talking and draining a sailboat
   d. working instead of sailing

The vowels "ai" makes the long /a/ sound in words like drain, proclaim, explain, and paint. Underline the "ai" vowel team in the words below.

Write rain proclaim times. Underline the vowel team.

Write plainly explain times. Underline the vowel team.

Write wait drain times. Underline the vowel team.

Write regain paint times. Underline the vowel team.

"ai" The Domain Name – Cloze Reading

Directions: Fill in the blanks with the correct "ai" word. Words may be used more than once.

Joe and Kyle like to sail. They sail every weekend. This weekend they were _____ sailing to Montauk.

There was a problem. They got to the boat. They found water. They found water at the bottom of the the sailboat.

"Must have been the rain," Joe said. "It has been _____ raining pretty hard."

"Or a hole," Kyle proclaimed.

"Pull the _____ drain and see what happens," Joe said.

"I'll tell you what happens. The boat will fill with water. The boat will fill with water if you pull the _____."

"Then why's there a _____ drain?" Joe asked.

"For when the boat's on land. The drain can only be pulled on land."

They got the boat out of the water. They pulled the drain. The boat was _____ draining. They looked over the boat. There were no holes. A little paint was chipped. But there were no holes.

"I'm not surprised. We _____ maintain our boat well," Kyle said.

"Let's get it back in the water. I'm ready for a sail. Aim for Montauk," Joe said.

"_____ aim for Montauk and let's go."

"It's too late. Looking for the hole took to long. I have to be back for work," Kyle said.

Word Bank			
sailing	drain	draining	drain
drain	raining	maintain	drain

Fluency Comprehension: "ai" The First Date

Directions: Please select the best response.

1. What did Maria do that AJ questioned?
   a. went to dinner with him
   b. wore braids
   c. ate a salad
   d. threw raisins

2. What is the theme or message in the reading?
   a. AJ and Maria have a great first date.
   b. AJ and Maria have a talk about a waitress in a restaurant.
   c. Maria throws raisins at a restaurant.
   d. AJ and Maria decide to go out again.

3. Read first paragraph. What is the best definition for the word complaint?
   a. protest
   b. praise
   c. grumble
   d. honor

4. In the reading, what is the best definition for the word proclaimed?
   a. said
   b. declared
   c. whispered
   d. hid

Directions: Say the word in your head as you color each word. Underline the "ai" vowel team.

complaint, WAITRESS, RAISINS, proclaimed, drain, AIM, braids, DRAIN, complaint, WAITRESS, RAISINS, proclaimed, drain, AIM, braids, DRAIN

"ai" The First Date – Cloze Reading

Directions: Fill in the blanks with the correct "ai" word. Words may be used more than once.

AJ and Maria were on a date. It was their first date. AJ tried to make everything great. And it started out fine. They went to a movie. They both loved it. Then they went to dinner. That's where things fell apart.

"I'm filing a _____ complaint," Maria said.

"Dinner was pretty bad," AJ said.

"Pretty bad? It was the worst," Maria _____ proclaimed.

"Well, not the worst."

"And the _____ waitress?" Maria exclaimed.

"The one with the braids in her hair?"

"Yes, the one with the _____ braids. I asked for no raisins. I wanted no _____ drain on my salad," Maria explained. "I hate raisins."

"I know. I was there," AJ said. "But you didn't have to throw them."

"My _____ aim was perfect."

"I hit the _____ drain with all but one," Maria said.

"You don't throw raisins in public," AJ said.

"The sink was right there. I had to aim for the drain. She asked for it. I asked for no _____ drain."

Word Bank			
drain	raisins	braids	aim
braids	waitress	proclaimed	complaint

Fluency Comprehension: "ai" The Big Win

Directions: Please select the best response.

1. What was the last thing Emma did?
   a. Exclaim "We won!"
   b. Join the team.
   c. Set the ball.
   d. Spike the ball.

2. What is the theme or message in the reading?
   a. winning and teamwork
   b. friendship and winning
   c. teamwork and friendship
   d. sportsmanship and teamwork

3. Read the first paragraph. What is the best definition for the word exclaimed?
   a. called out
   b. whispered
   c. cried
   d. said

4. In the reading, what is the best definition for the word refrain?
   a. keep going
   b. hold back or stop
   c. move forward
   d. chorus of a song

Directions: Say the word in your head as you color each word. Underline the "ai" vowel team.

faith, NAILED, pain, GAIN, refrain, REMAIN, contain, faith, NAILED, pain, GAIN, refrain, REMAIN, contain, faith, NAILED, pain, GAIN, refrain, REMAIN, contain

---

Fluency Comprehension: "ai" The Domain Name

Directions: Please select the best response.

1. What did Danny and Jake regain?
   a. only their website
   b. their domain name
   c. their prepaid phone
   d. their business

2. What did Danny and Jake upload?
   a. their domain name and their website
   b. their brand
   c. their domain name
   d. their website

3. Re-read the sentence: "It was written plainly on paper." What does the word plainly mean?
   a. clearly
   b. directly
   c. barely
   d. bluntly

4. What is the reading mostly about?
   a. a domain name
   b. brothers who get their website back
   c. brothers who get their domain name back
   d. none of the above

The vowels "ai" makes the long /a/ sound in words like domain, plainly, mail, and regain. Underline the "ai" vowel team in the words below.

Write rain domain times. Underline the vowel team.

Write plainly three times. Underline the vowel team.

Write wait mail times. Underline the vowel team.

Write regain three times. Underline the vowel team.

"ai" The Domain Name – Cloze Reading

Directions: Fill in the blanks with the correct "ai" word. Words may be used more than once.

Danny ran to the door. He grabbed the mail.

"Let me see," Jake said. Jake was his brother. "I wanted to look first."

"You move like a snail. I got here first. I'll open the _____ mail," Danny said.

"Is it there? Did we _____ regain the domain?" Jake asked.

"I don't know," Danny said.

"Well, look through the _____," Jake said.

They were talking about their _____ domain name. They owned a website. Then, they lost the name. Now, they were trying to get it back.

"Here it is. A balance remains, but we got it back."

"I thought we prepaid for the website? I thought we _____ prepaid the domain?"

"We prepaid most of it," Danny said. "We paid enough. It's ours again."

There it was. It was written _____ plainly on the paper. They did it. They got their domain name back.

"Yep, plain as day. Now, we can start branding our name," Jake said.

They'd been waiting a long time for this. Now they had it. They had their _____ domain name back.

"Let's not waste another minute. Let's go upload our logo," Danny said.

"Let's upload our whole website," Jake said. "Then we'll put it out on social media."

Their website was up within an hour. Their business was booming within a week.

Word Bank			
regain	mail	domain	prepaid
domain	domain	plainly	snail

Name: _____   Number: _____

Word Search

Directions: Find the "ai" words. The words can be up or down, left to right, or diagonal.

Word Bank

detail	waiting	rain	remain	maintain	proclaim	stain	exclaim
waiting	gained	rainy	domain	attain	braids	draining	main
soil	fail	plainly	train	stain	rainy	faithful	frail

Complete the crossword puzzle below

Across

1. A hairstyle; interwoven strands of hair (**braid**)
4. A fall of water from the sky. (**rain**)
5. To call out. (**proclaim**)
8. To keep up or carry on; continue. (**maintain**)
9. To tell all about something. (**explain**)

Down

2. A part of something d___ l___ l. (**detail**)
3. To protest against something or someone. (**complain**)
4. To stain in one place. (**remain**)
6. In a plain manner. (**plainly**)
7. To discolor, get dirty, or spot. (**stain**)

Name: _____   Number: _____

Word Maze

Directions: Follow the "ai" words to the END. You may move up and down or left and right.

START	rain	main	play	day	may	pay
stay	bay	faithful	way	ray	say	clay
spray	pray	rainy	display	sleep	agree	guarantee
claim	aim	maintain	today	display	array	today
gain	sleep	delay	relay	holiday	essay	betrayal
pain	deep	haystack	way	employee	steep	queen
waiting	plainly	domain	afraid	pray	saying	display
breeze	payable	may	prepaid	read	bread	breed
feed	horse	house	sail	zookeeper	volunteer	employee
degree	spray	guarantee	draining	exclaim	peace	peaceful
feature	trainee	teenager	clean	frail	beneath	decrease
reason	zookeeper	season	engineer	raisin	see	tree
feel	sleepover	season	reason	attain	teach	creature
theater	queen	beaver	degree	paint	contain	waitress
beaver	freeze	overseen	cheer	beneath	beach	rain
beat	meat	read	feed	speak	weave	END

Phonics for Older Students

Long /ā/

Vowel Team ay

Two Pencils and a Book

Multi-syllable Digraphs

Teach one vowel team at a time. This is especially important for struggling readers. Focus on one pattern for at least 2 or 3 days until students can recognize the vowel team easily without prompting. Some students will need a week or longer. **Start with one syllable words** then move on to multisyllabic words.

The following worksheet – "Syllable Division" is a guided exercise to use with the Presentation; however, if you are working with one student or a small group of students – you can just use the script as guided practice. If your students have more advanced decoding skills, you may move directly to the fluency exercises.

The script for the presentation and worksheet is written in the "Notes" section of the presentation. It is basically…

- The word is display.
- Underline the vowels.
- Put your hand on your chin.
- Each time your chin moves, you are reading a new syllable.
- Now I am going to say the word. You will say it after me.
- "display"
- Students repeat.
- How many times did your chin move? (2)
- Good. How many syllables are in display? (2)
- Great. Now put a line through the syllables.

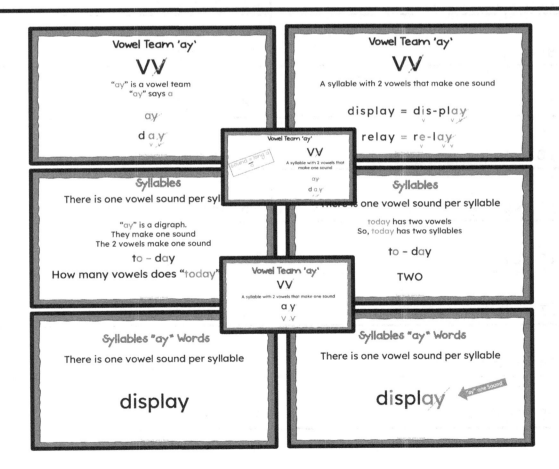

Syllable Division

1. display	16. yesterday
2. day	17. delay
3. may	18. relay
4. pay	19. holiday
5. stay	20. essay
6. bay	21. betrayal
7. way	22. bayonet
8. ray	23. sway
9. say	24. displayed
10. clay	25. haystack
11. spray	26. mayonnaise
12. pray	27. payable
13. play	28. praying
14. tray	29. sayings
15. today	30. away

Name: _____ Number: _____

Test Date 1: _____ Test Date 2: _____

Long A 'ay' Vowel Team
Teacher Page

Teacher Say: Put your finger on the first word. We are going to read down the column. Read each word. Begin.

Word	Correct	Word	Correct
play		yesterday	
day		delay	
may		relay	
pay		holiday	
stay		essay	
bay		betrayal	
way		bayonet	
ray		allay	
say		displayed	
clay		haystack	
spray		mayonnaise	
pray		payable	
display		praying	
array		sayings	
today		away	

Name: _____ Number: _____

Test Date 1: _____ Test Date 2: _____

Digraph with "ay"
Student Page

Word	Word
play	yesterday
day	delay
may	relay
pay	holiday
stay	essay
bay	betrayal
way	bayonet
ray	sway
say	displayed
clay	haystack
spray	mayonnaise
pray	payable
display	praying
tray	sayings
today	away

Vowel Team "ay" - Interactive Notebook Page

Vowel Team "ay"

Digraph "ay"

A digraph is **two letters that make one sound.**

Write each word on a flower stem.
play, day, may, pay, stay, bay, way, ray, say, clay, spray, pray, display, tray, today, yesterday, delay, relay, holiday, essay, betrayal, bayonet, sway, displayed, haystack, mayonnaise, payable, praying, saying, away.

Word Pocket – "ay" Set 1

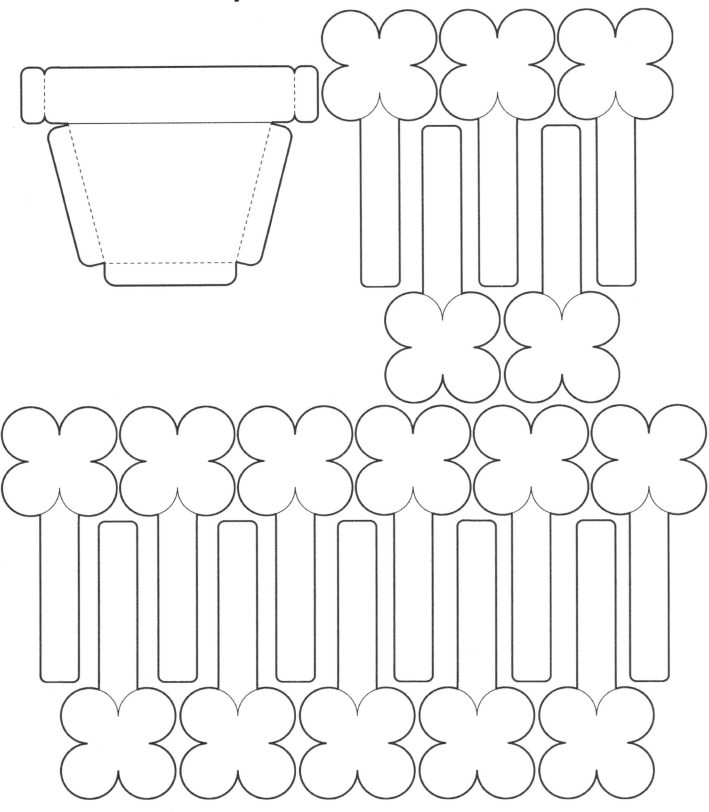

Put word on each slide of the flower. Cut out. Paste the pocket to your notebook and fill the pot with flowers. **Words:** play, day, may, pay, stay, bay, way, ray, say, clay, spray, pray, display, tray, today.

Long A 'ay' Vowel Team – Cloze the Gap

A digraph is **two letters that make one sound.**
Directions: Use the words from the word bank to complete the sentences.

1. We want to _____ on the playground.

2. The last _____ of sunshine shined through the window.

3. What _____ is your birthday?

4. What did dad _____ ? Can we go play?

5. _____ I have a cupcake please?

6. We made vases out of _____ .

7. Do you have the money to _____ for the tickets?

8. _____ in your seats until the bus stops.

9. The candy _____ won first prize.

10. The boat sailed on the _____ .

11. Fill your _____ with your lunch.

12. Turn around; we are going the wrong _____ .

13. That happened yesterday. This is _____ .

Word Bank						
play	day	may	pay	stay	bay	way
ray	say	clay	pray	display	tray	today

Sentence Fluency: 'ay' – Passage 11

Go play on the playground.	05
Let's go play on the playground.	11
It is a great day to play on the playground.	21
Today is a great day to play on the playground.	31
Look at the rays of sunshine on the playground.	40
What do you say?	44
What do you say we play, and then we pay for ice cream?	57
We stayed at the playground most of the day.	66
On the way home, we stopped for ice cream.	75
On the way to pay for ice cream we looked at a display.	88
The display was about boating on the bay.	96
The bay was only two miles away.	103
Let's go play at the bay on Saturday.	111
Let's go play at the bay while the sun rays are out.	123
We may go to the bay on Saturday.	131
We may go to the bay on Saturday and play in the waves.	144
This day we will stay in town.	151
This day we will stay in town and play with clay.	162
Put the tray away.	166
Put the tray from our ice cream dishes away.	175
Put the tray from our ice cream away so we can play with clay.	189
All in all, it was a great day.	197

Words Read: _____	Words Read: _____	Words Read: _____
minus mistakes: _____	minus mistakes: _____	minus mistakes: _____
equals wpms: _____	equals wpms: _____	equals wpms: _____

Name: _____ Number: _____

Fluency: 'ay' May's Day – 325L – Passage 12

Once upon a time, there was a girl named May. May woke up one day	15
feeling happy. May was happy because it was a beautiful day. She wanted to	29
go out and play. Her mom said she had to stay. May had to clean her room	46
before she could play.	50
May went to her room. She cleaned it up. She put her stuff away. Then she	66
saw a small piece of clay on her shelf. She began to play with the clay.	82
While she was playing with the clay, she heard her mom say, "May, it's	96
time to go out and play. It's time to go out and play at the bay."	112
May was so excited. She put the clay away. She ran all the way to the bay.	129
May loved the bay. She saw a ray swimming in the water. May was so	144
excited to see the ray. She jumped up and down. She started to spray water	159
everywhere.	160
Her friend Ray ran up to May. "May, stop spraying water. You're getting	173
people wet!"	175
May stopped spraying water. She started to play in the sand. She built a	189
big display out of the sand.	195
"May, that's a cool display. Let's put it on a tray. You can take it home,"	211
said Ray.	213
May carried the tray home. May put the tray on display in her room. May	228
smiled. She was glad for the fun day.	236

Words Read: _____	Words Read: _____	Words Read: _____
minus mistakes: _____	minus mistakes: _____	minus mistakes: _____
equals wpms: _____	equals wpms: _____	equals wpms: _____

Name: _____ Number: _____

Fluency Comprehension: 'ay' May's Day

Directions: Please select the best response.

1. What was May doing when she was told she could go outside?
   a. eating breakfast
   b. playing with clay
   c. feeding her ray
   d. talking on the phone

2. Who told May to stop spraying water?
   a. her mom
   b. her day
   c. Jay
   d. Ray

3. Write a sentience using the words play, tray and stay.

   _____

   _____

   _____

4. Read the sentence: "May was so excited to play." Excited means:
   a. nervous and anxious
   b. thrilled and happy
   c. upset and sad
   d. cool and calm

5. In the sentence: "May, stop spraying water," what is the best definition of the word spraying?
   a. drying
   b. gushing
   c. squirting
   d. rubbing

6. What did May carry home?
   a. her friend Ray
   b. nothing
   c. seashells
   d. a tray

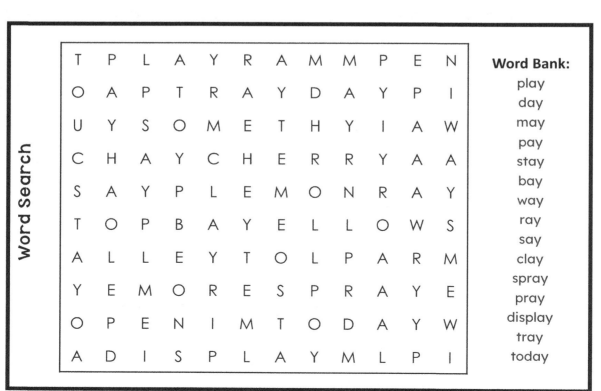

Word Search

T	P	L	A	Y	R	A	M	M	P	E	N
O	A	P	T	R	A	Y	D	A	Y	P	I
U	Y	S	O	M	E	T	H	Y	I	A	W
C	H	A	Y	C	H	E	R	R	Y	A	A
S	A	Y	P	L	E	M	O	N	R	A	Y
T	O	P	B	A	Y	E	L	L	O	W	S
A	L	L	E	Y	T	O	L	P	A	R	M
Y	E	M	O	R	E	S	P	R	A	Y	E
O	P	E	N	I	M	T	O	D	A	Y	W
A	D	I	S	P	L	A	Y	M	L	P	I

Word Bank:
play
day
may
pay
stay
bay
way
ray
say
clay
spray
pray
display
tray
today

Name: _____ Number: _____

'ay' May's Day – Cloze Reading

Directions: Fill in the blanks with the correct "ay" word. Words may be used more than once.

Once upon a time, there was a girl named May. May woke up one _____

feeling happy. May was happy because it was a beautiful day. She wanted to go out and

play. Her mom said she had to _____ . May had to clean her room before she

could play.

May went to her room. She cleaned it up. She put her stuff _____. Then she

saw a small piece of _____ on her shelf. She began to _____ with the

clay.

While she was playing with the clay, she heard her mom _____, "May, it's time

to go out and play. It's time to go out and play at the _____. We'll play on the

beach."

May was so excited. She put the _____ away. She ran all the way to the bay.

May loved the bay. She saw a ray swimming in the water. May was so excited to see

the _____. She jumped up and down. She started to spray water everywhere.

Her friend Ray ran up to May. "May, stop spraying water. You're getting people wet!"

May stopped _____ water. She started to play in the sand. She built a big

display out of the sand.

"May, that's a cool _____. Let's put it on a tray. You can take it home," said

Ray.

May carried the _____ home. May put the tray on display in her room. May

smiled. She was glad for the fun day.

Word Bank						
tray	display	spraying	ray	clay	bay	clay
	play	away	stay	day	say	

Name: _____ Number: _____

Sentence Fluency: 'ay' A Day to Play – 325L – Passage 13

Today is a day to play! You may pick any way you want to play. You may	17
stay inside. You may stay inside and play with clay. You may go outside and	32
play by the bay.	36
If you stay inside, you may make things with clay. You may make a	50
display for your toys. You may make a tray for your snacks. If you play	65
outside, you could play in the spray by the bay. You may even see a ray. You	82
may even see a ray in the bay.	90
Make sure to have fun. Make sure you enjoy your day.	101
You can say "yay!" You can say "yay!" because it's a great day to play.	116
Remember, you may need to pay attention to the rules. If you go to the	131
bay, you may play. You may play, if you follow the rules. If you go to the	148
bay, pay attention to the rules.	154
So go ahead and play! And remember to have a great day.	166

Words Read: _____	Words Read: _____	Words Read: _____
minus mistakes: _____	minus mistakes: _____	minus mistakes: _____
equals wpms: _____	equals wpms: _____	equals wpms: _____

Fluency Comprehension: "ay" A Day to Play

Directions: Please select the best response.

1. Read the first paragraph. What is one listed to play?
   a. outside with a ray
   b. outside with clay
   c. outside at the bay
   d. inside with My

2. What must you pay attention to?
   a. the bay
   b. Ray
   c. the waves at the bay
   d. the rules at the bay

3. Write a sentience using the words bay, way, stay.

   _____
   _____
   _____

Directions: Unscramble the words below.

8. lapy   _____

9. sidaypl   _____

10. lacy   _____

11. datoy   _____

4. Read the sentence: "Pay attention to the rules." Attention means:
   a. be interested in
   b. mind
   c. forget
   d. help

5. In the sentence: "You may see a ray at the bay," what is the best definition of the word ray?
   a. the sun
   b. a type of sandcastle
   c. sunglasses
   d. a sea creature

6. According to the reading, what can you make things out of?
   a. clay
   b. sand
   c. rays
   d. trays

play, day, may, pay, stay, bay, way, ray, say, clay, spray, pray, display, tray, today

Name: _____ Number: _____

'ay' May's Day – Cloze Reading

Directions: Fill in the blanks with the correct 'ay' word. Words may be used more than once.

_____ is a day to play! You may pick any way you want to play. You may

stay inside. You may _____ inside and play with clay. You may go outside and

play by the bay.

If you stay inside, you may make things with _____ . You may make a display

for your toys. You may make a _____ for your snacks. If you play outside, you

could play in the _____ by the bay. You may even see a ray. You may even see

a ray in the bay.

Make sure to have fun. Make sure you enjoy your _____ .

You can say "yay!" You can say "yay!" because it's a great day to _____ .

Remember, you may need to pay attention to the rules. If you go to the bay. If you

go to the bay, _____ attention to the rules.

So go ahead and play! And remember to have a great day.

Word Bank			
pay	day	play	spray
tray	stay	clay	today

Word Pocket – 'ay''' Set 2

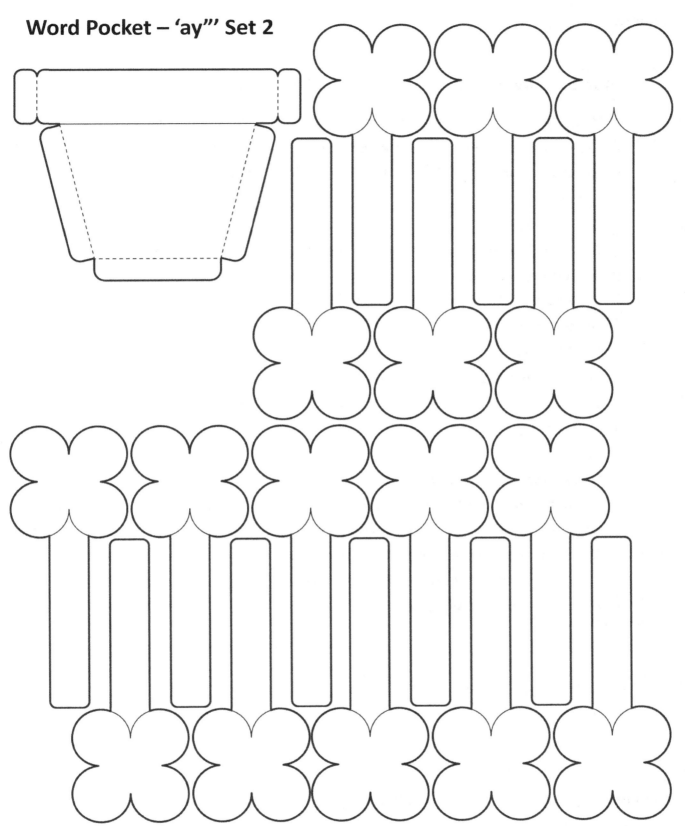

Put word on each slide of the flower. Cut out. Paste the pocket to your notebook and fill the pot with flowers. Words: yesterday, delay, relay, holiday, essay, betrayal, bayonet, sway, displayed, haystack, mayonnaise, payable, praying, saying, away.

Fluency: 'ay' Set 2 – 350L – Jay's Essay – Passage 14

Yesterday was a holiday. I couldn't play. I had to finish my essay. I was	15
praying that I would get it done early. But there was a delay. My computer	30
crashed. I had to write it by hand. I was starting to sway back and forth in	47
my chair.	49
"Why today?"	51
Just then, my little brother came in. He displayed his toy soldiers. He had	65
them fighting with bayonets.	69
"Jay be quiet." I said to my brother. "I have to finish my essay."	83
He kept playing.	86
I felt betrayed.	89
Finally, I finished my essay. I put it away.	98
I went outside to play baseball. I saw a haystack next to the ball field. It	114
looked like a great place to play.	121
"Jay," I called. "Come play!"	126
"Play later," Mom called. "It's time for lunch."	134
My mom made sandwiches with turkey and mayonnaise.	142
"Ray? Will you play soldiers with me?"	149
"Sure Jay. Let's bring them to the haystack."	157
"That's a great way to play with them today," he said.	168
It was a great day. We sure do like holidays.	178

Words Read: _____	Words Read: _____	Words Read: _____
minus mistakes: _____	minus mistakes: _____	minus mistakes: _____
equals wpms: _____	equals wpms: _____	equals wpms: _____

Fluency Comprehension: 'ay Set 2 – Jay's Essay

Directions: Please select the best response.

1. What did Jay have to finish he could play?
   a. cleaning his room
   b. fixing his computer
   c. bucking hay
   d. writing his essay

2. Where did Ray and Jay play?
   a. in Ray's room
   b. in Jay's room
   c. on the haystack
   d. at the ball field.

3. Write a sentience using the words holiday, essay and displayed.

   _____
   _____
   _____

4. Read third paragraph. What is the best definition for the word "<u>displayed</u>?"
   a. put on a shelf
   b. shown on a computer
   c. shown
   d. laid out

5. What kind of sandwiches did mom make?
   a. turkey and mayonnaise
   b. ham and mayonnaise
   c. cheese and mayonnaise
   d. salami and mayonnaise

6. List important details from the story?

   _____
   _____
   _____

Word Search

Y	E	S	T	E	R	D	A	Y	S	P	A
A	P	R	A	Y	I	N	G	P	P	H	W
M	A	Y	O	N	N	A	I	S	E	O	A
L	Y	E	R	E	L	A	Y	A	M	L	Y
B	A	Y	B	A	Y	O	N	E	T	I	S
L	B	E	T	R	A	Y	A	L	J	D	D
U	L	I	P	S	W	A	T	Y	A	A	E
E	E	S	S	A	Y	E	T	I	L	Y	L
D	I	S	P	L	A	Y	E	D	E	K	A
U	P	H	A	Y	S	T	A	C	K	A	Y

Word Bank:
yesterday
delay
relay
holiday
essay
betrayal
bayonet
sway
displayed
haystack
mayonnaise
payable
praying
away

'ay' Jay's Essay – Cloze Reading

Directions: Fill in the blanks with the correct "ay" word. Words may be used more than once.

Yesterday was a _____. I couldn't play. I had to finish my essay. I was

praying that I could get it done early. But there was a _____ . My computer

crashed. I had to write it by hand. I was starting to sway back and forth in my chair.

"Why today?"

Just then, my little brother came in. He _____ his toy soldiers. He had them

fighting with bayonets.

"Jay be quiet." I said to my brother. "I have to finish my _____."

He kept _____ .

I felt like betrayed me.

Finally, I finished my essay. I put it away

I went outside to play baseball. I saw a _____ next to the ball field. It looked

like a great place to play.

"Jay," I called. "Come play!"

"Play later," Mom called. "It's time for lunch."

My mom made sandwiches with turkey and _____.

"Ray? Will you play soldiers with me?"

"Sure Jay. Let's bring them to the haystack."

"That's a great way to play with them today," he said.

It was a great day. We sure do like _____.

Word Bank			
holidays	essay	haystack	delay
mayonnaise	displayed	delay	holiday

Fluency: "ay" Set 2 – May and the Soldiers– 350L – Passage 15

Yesterday was a holiday. May wanted to play at the bay. She had been	14
counting down the days for this break from school. Her plans were met with	28
a delay. She had an essay due the next day.	38
May was feeling betrayed by herself for putting it off. She wanted to	51
play. Only she knew she had to work on her essay. She sat down to write.	67
She heard noises outside. She looked out the window. She saw soldiers	79
marching towards her house. They had bayonets in their hands.	89
May didn't know what to do. She hid in a haystack in her backyard. May	104
heard one of the soldiers relay a message. He was saying that they were	118
looking for their lost dog, Jay. He'd run off from the base.	130
May walked to the street.	135
"I'll relay your message," May said. "I hope you find your dog."	147
"Thank you," the soldiers said. "He's a lab. He likes to eat mayonnaise."	160
Then they went away.	164
"Mayonnaise! That's bad for dogs to eat," May thought.	173
May went up and down her block. May relayed the message. Then she	186
went back to her essay.	191
It took her most of the day to write her essay. Finally, she finished. She	206
joined her family at the bay.	212
She told her family about the soldiers. "They had bayonets. They were	224
looking for their dog. He likes mayonnaise."	231
"Cool," said her brother Ray. "Now, let's play."	239

Words Read: _____	Words Read: _____	Words Read: _____
minus mistakes: _____	minus mistakes: _____	minus mistakes: _____
equals wpms: _____	equals wpms: _____	equals wpms: _____

Name: _____ Number: _____

Fluency Comprehension: 'ay' May and the Soldiers

Directions: Please select the best response.

1. What did May see on the streets?
   a. a dog with mayonnaise
   b. a haystack
   c. a jar of mayonnaise
   d. soldiers with bayonets

2. What is the correct order?
   a. May finishes her essay, she sees soldiers, then she goes to the bay
   b. May sees soldiers, she goes to the bay, she finishes her essay
   c. May sees soldiers, she goes up and down her block, she goes to the bay
   d. May goes to the bay, she sees soldiers, she finishes her essay

3. Re-read the sentence: "Her plans were met with a <u>delay</u>." Which word could you use in place of <u>delay</u>?
   a. stall
   b. party
   c. note
   d. prayer

4. In the sentence: "May heard one of the soldiers <u>relaying</u> a message," what is the best definition of the word <u>relaying</u>?
   a. telling
   b. passing on
   c. giving out
   d. taking back

Write mayonnaise three times. Underline the vowel team.

_____   _____   _____

Write relaying three times. Underline the vowel team.

_____   _____   _____

Write delay three times. Underline the vowel team.

_____   _____   _____

Write bayonet three times. Underline the vowel team.

_____   _____   _____

Name: _____ Number: _____

'ay' May and the Soldiers – Cloze Reading

Directions: Fill in the blanks with the correct "ay" word. Words may be used more than once.

Yesterday was a _____. May wanted to play at the bay. She had been

counting down the days for this break from school. Her plans were met with a

_____. She had an essay due the next day.

May was feeling betrayed by herself for putting it off. She wanted to play. Only she

knew she had to work on her _____. She sat down to write. She heard noises

outside. She looked out the window. She saw soldiers marching towards her house. They

had _____ in their hands.

May didn't know what to do. She hid in a haystack in her backyard. May heard one of

the soldiers _____ a message. He was saying that they were looking for their

lost dog, Jay. He'd run off from the base.

May walked to the street.

"I'll _____ your message," May said. "I hope you find your dog."

"Thank you," the soldiers said. "He's a lab. He likes to eat creamy _____."

Then they went _____.

"Mayonnaise! That's bad for dogs to eat," May thought.

May went up and down her block. May relayed the message. Then she went back to

her essay.

Word Bank			
away	relaying	essay	delay
mayonnaise	bayonets	holiday	relay

Name: _____ Number: _____

Fluency: 'ay' All – Lexile 375L – Passage 16

Ray liked to play at the bay. He loved to play in the sand every day. He	17
loved building sandcastles and making clay figures. Ray would stay until the	29
sun began to sway in the sky. That's when his mother would call him away.	44
Ray's mother would call him away for dinner.	52
One day, Ray went to the beach with his tray. His tray was full of toys. He	69
also had spray bottles to spray. He got to the beach. Someone was playing	83
in his spot. Ray was upset. Now, he had to delay his playtime.	96
Ray found a new spot to play and display his work. He sprayed his sand	111
art with water. A girl named May came to the beach. May loved to play in	127
the sand too. She asked Ray if she could play. Ray was happy to have a	143
friend to play with. They spent the rest of the day in the sand. They also	159
created clay figures.	162
The next day, Ray woke up early. He was excited to play with May again.	177
He went to the beach. May was not there. He waited and waited. May did	192
not come. Ray was worried May might be sick. He went to her house. May's	197
mom told him May had gone on holiday.	205
Ray was sad. He would not get to play with May. But he decided to write	222
her an essay. The essay was about how much fun they had playing on the	237
beach. He also included a small betrayal of how sad he was. He was sad	252
that she was not there to play with him.	261

Words Read: _____	Words Read: _____	Words Read: _____
minus mistakes: _____	minus mistakes: _____	minus mistakes: _____
equals wpms: _____	equals wpms: _____	equals wpms: _____

Name: _____ Number: _____

'ay' All – Cloze Reading

Directions: Fill in the blanks with the correct "ay" word. Words may be used more than once.

Ray liked to play at the _____. He loved to play in the sand every day. He loved building sandcastles and making clay figures. Ray would often stay until the sun began to _____ in the sky. That's when his mother would call him away. His mother would call him away for dinner.

One day, Ray went to the beach with his _____ of toys. He also had spray bottles to spray. He got to the beach. Someone was _____ on the beach in his spot. Ray was upset because he had to delay his playtime.

After a while, Ray found a new spot to play and display his work. He sprayed his sand art with water. A girl named May came to the beach. May loved to play in the sand too. She asked Ray if she could join him. Ray was happy to have a friend to play with. They spent the rest of the _____ making castles. They also creating _____ figures.

The next day, Ray woke up early. He was excited to _____ with May again. But when he got to the beach, she was not there. He waited and waited. May did not come. Ray was worried that she might be sick. So, he went to her house to check on her. When got there, May's mom told him that May had gone on _____.

Word Bank – Some Words May Not Be Used						
play	day	may	pay	stay	bay	way
ray	say	clay	pray	display	tray	today
yesterday	delay	relay	holiday	essay	bayonet	betrayal
sway	displayed	haystack	mayonnaise	payable	praying	away

Long A 'ay' Word Maze

Directions: Follow the 'ay' words to the END. You may move up and down or left and right.

START	great	wait	bait	the	and	holiday
play	day	may	holiday	got	way	stay
wish	miss	float	display	tray	some	today
praying	tray	way	today	boat	float	display
fix	bayonet	go	too	sleep	away	meet
box	betrayal	haystack	say	same	payable	greet
boat	goat	note	delay	why	bay	meat
betrayal	fame	praying	way	silver	the	rain
stay	gold	away	plane	plain	fish	beat
wish	treat	bay	stay	delay	relay	payable
fleet	why	stuff	rough	pass	past	tray
blue	red	read	tray	play	away	clay
said	roam	bone	display	phone	tone	next
mane	name	stop	essay	today	play	day
tray	some	today	march	soldier	fold	may
boat	float	display	pool	house	rust	END

Long A 'ay' Crosswords

Directions: Fill out the crossword by answering the questions.

Across

3. a blade made to fit the muzzle end of a rifle

6. a period of 24 hours

7. egg yolks and oil and vinegar

10. at or to a distance in space or time

12. a short piece of writing on a specific subject

14. money that is due for work done

15. to remain

Down

1. something you mold

2. a day with no work or school

4. a shallow flat thing to carry stuff on

5. a stack of hay

6. to make late or slow

8. to be allowed or permitted to do

9. yesterday, _____ , and tomorrow

11. something you do for fun

13. to swing back and forth

'ay' Story Strips

GOAL: To gain a better understanding

Directions for Classroom Use: Cut the sentence strips and assemble them into a complete story.

"Yesterday was a holiday," Ray answered. "I wanted to play in the bay on my holiday."
Only this day was different. It was Saturday. Ray had to stay home. Ray had to stay home and finish his essay
Ray sighed. He finished his essay without delay and dreamed about next Saturday.
"Ray," his mom said. "You betrayed yourself. You should have finished your essay yesterday."
Ray did not want to stay home. He did not want to finish his essay. He wanted to go to the bay. He wanted to feel the ocean spray.
"Well," Mom said. "That means today you stay home. You can always go to the bay next Saturday."
Once upon a time, there was a boy named Ray. Ray liked to play by the bay. Each weekend he went to play by the bay. He went without delay.

Worksheet 1 — Digraph "ay" One – Cloze the Gap

Name: _____ Number: _____

Digraph "ay" One - Cloze the Gap

A digraph is two letters that make one sound.

Directions: Use the words from the word bank to complete the sentences.

1. We want to __play__ on the playground.
2. The last __ray__ of sunshine shined through the window.
3. What __day__ is your birthday?
4. What did dad __say__? Can we go play?
5. __May__ I have a cupcake please?
6. We made vases out of __clay__.
7. Do you have the money to __pay__ for the tickets?
8. __Stay__ in your seats until the bus stops.
9. The candy __display__ won first prize.
10. The boat sailed on the __bay__.
11. Fill your __tray__ with your lunch.
12. Turn around, we are going the wrong __way__.
13. That happened yesterday. This is __today__.

Word Bank

play	day	may	pay	stay	bay	way
ray	say	clay	pray	display	tray	today

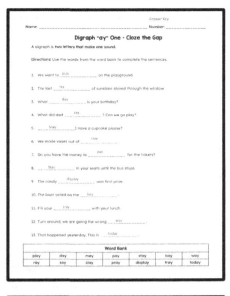

Worksheet 2 — Fluency Comprehension: "ay" May's Day

Name: _____ Number: _____

Fluency Comprehension: "ay" May's Day

Directions: Please select the best response.

1. What was May doing when she was told she could go outside?
   a. eating breakfast
   b. playing with clay
   c. feeding her ray
   d. talking on her phone

2. Who told May to stop spraying water?
   a. her mom
   b. her day
   c. Jay
   d. Ray

3. Write a sentence using the words play, tray and stay.

4. Read the sentence: "May was so excited to play." Excited means:
   a. nervous and anxious
   b. thrilled and happy
   c. upset and sad
   d. cool and calm

5. In the sentence: "May, stop spraying water," what is the best definition of the word spraying?
   a. drying
   b. gushing
   c. squirting
   d. rubbing

6. What did May carry home?
   a. her friend Ray
   b. nothing
   c. seashells
   d. a tray

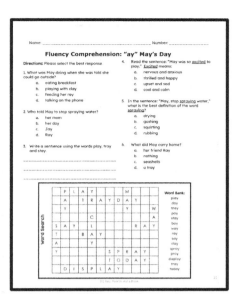

Word Bank: play, day, may, pay, stay, bay, ray, say, clay, spray, pray, display, tray, today

Worksheet 3 — "ay" May's Day – Cloze Reading

Name: _____ Number: _____

"ay" May's Day – Cloze Reading

Directions: Fill in the blanks with the correct "ay" word. Words may be used more than once.

Once upon a time, there was a girl named May. May woke up one __day__ feeling happy. May was happy because it was a beautiful day. She wanted to go out and play. Her mom said she had to __stay__. May had to clean her room before she could play.

May went to her room. She cleaned it up. She put her stuff __away__. Then she saw a small piece of __clay__ on her shelf. She began to __play__ with the clay.

While she was playing with the clay, she heard her mom __say__, "May, it's time to go out and play. It's time to go out and play at the __bay__. We'll play on the beach."

May was so excited. She put the __clay__ away. She ran all the way to the bay. May loved the bay. She saw a ray swimming in the water. May was so excited to see the __ray__. She jumped up and down. She started to spray water everywhere. Her friend Ray ran up to May. "May, stop spraying water. You're getting people wet!"

May stopped __spraying__ water. She started to play in the sand. She built a big display out of the sand.

"May, that's so cool __display__. Let's put it on a tray. You can take it home," said Ray.

May carried the __tray__ home. May put the tray on display in her room. May smiled. She was glad for the fun day.

Word Bank

tray	display	spraying	ray	clay	bay	clay
play	away	stay	day	say		

Worksheet 4 — Fluency Comprehension: "ay" A Day to Play

Name: _____ Number: _____

Fluency Comprehension: "ay" A Day to Play

Directions: Please select the best response.

1. Read the first paragraph. What is one listed to play?
   a. outside with a ray
   b. outside with clay
   c. outside at the bay
   d. inside with My

2. What must you pay attention to?
   a. the bay
   b. Ray
   c. the waves at the bay
   d. the rules of the bay

3. Write a sentence using the words bay, way, stay.

Directions: Unscramble the words below.

8. lapy __play__
9. sidaypl __display__
10. lacy __clay__
11. datoy __today__

4. Read the sentence: "Pay attention to the rules." Attention means:
   a. be interested in
   b. mind
   c. forget
   d. help

5. In the sentence: "You may see a ray at the bay," what is the best definition of the word ray?
   a. the sun
   b. a type of sandcastle
   c. sunglasses
   d. a sea creature

6. According to the reading, what can you make things out of?
   a. clay
   b. sand
   c. rays
   d. trays

play, clay, may, pay, stay, bay, way, ray, say, clay, spray, pray, display, tray, today

Worksheet 5 — "ay" May's Day – Cloze Reading

Name: _____ Number: _____

"ay" May's Day – Cloze Reading

Directions: Fill in the blanks with the correct "ay" word. Words may be used more than once.

__today__ is a day to play! You may pick any way you want to play. You may stay inside. You may __stay__ inside and play with clay. You may go outside and play by the bay.

If you stay inside, you may make things with __clay__. You may make a display for your toys. You may make a __tray__ for your snacks. If you play outside, you could play in the __spray__ by the bay. You may even see a ray. You may even see a ray in the bay.

Make sure to have fun. Make sure you enjoy your __day__.

You can say "yay!" You can say "yay" because it's a great day to __play__.

Remember, you may need to pay attention to the rules. If you go to the bay. If you go to the bay, __pay__ attention to the rules.

So go ahead and play! And remember to have a great day.

Word Bank

pay	day	play	spray
tray	stay	clay	today

Worksheet 6 — Fluency Comprehension: "ay" Set 2 – Jay's Essay

Name: _____ Number: _____

Fluency Comprehension: "ay" Set 2 – Jay's Essay

Directions: Please select the best response.

1. What did Jay have to finish so he could play?
   a. cleaning his room
   b. fixing his computer
   c. bucking hay
   d. writing his essay

2. Where did Ray and Jay play?
   a. in Ray's room
   b. in Jay's room
   c. on the haystack
   d. at the ball field

3. Write a sentence using the words holiday, essay and displayed.

4. Read the third paragraph. What is the best definition for the word "displayed?"
   a. put on a shelf
   b. shown on a computer
   c. shown
   d. laid out

5. What kind of sandwiches did mom make?
   a. turkey and mayonnaise
   b. ham and mayonnaise
   c. cheese and mayonnaise
   d. salami and mayonnaise

6. What important details can you remember from the story?

Word Bank: yesterday, delay, relay, holiday, essay, betrayal, sway, displayed, haystack, mayonnaise, payable, praying, away

Worksheet 7 — "ay" Jay's Essay – Cloze Reading

Name: _____ Number: _____

"ay" Jay's Essay – Cloze Reading

Directions: Fill in the blanks with the correct "ay" word. Words may be used more than once.

Yesterday was a __holiday__. I couldn't play. I had to finish my essay. I was praying that I could get it done early. But there was a __delay__. My computer crashed. I had to write it by hand. I was starting to sway back and forth in my chair.

"Why today?"

Just then, my little brother came in. He __displayed__ his toy soldiers. He had them fighting with bayonets.

"Jay, be quiet," I said to my brother. "I have to finish my __essay__."

He kept __playing__.

I felt like betrayed me.

Finally, I finished my essay. I put it away.

I went outside to play baseball. I saw a __haystack__ next to the ball field. It looked like a great place to play.

"Jay," I called. "Come play!"

"Play later," Mom called. "It's time for lunch."

My mom made sandwiches with turkey and __mayonnaise__.

"Ray? Will you play soldiers with me?"

"Sure Jay. Let's bring them to the haystack."

"That's a great way to play with them today," he said.

It was a great day. We sure do like __holidays__.

Word Bank

holidays	essay	haystack	delay
mayonnaise	displayed	delay	holiday

Worksheet 8 — Fluency Comprehension: "ay" May and the Soldiers

Name: _____ Number: _____

Fluency Comprehension: "ay" May and the Soldiers

Directions: Please select the best response.

1. What did May see on the streets?
   a. a dog with mayonnaise
   b. a haystack
   c. a jar of mayonnaise
   d. soldiers with bayonets

2. What is the correct order?
   a. May finishes her essay, she goes to the bay
   b. May sees soldiers, she goes to the bay, she finishes her essay
   c. May sees soldiers, she goes up and down her block, she goes to the bay
   d. May goes to the bay, she sees soldiers, she finishes her essay

3. Write a sentence using the words mayonnaise, sway, and essay.

4. Re-read the sentence: "Her plans were met with a delay." Which word could you use in place of delay?
   a. stall
   b. party
   c. note
   d. prayer

5. In the sentence: "May heard one of the soldiers relaying a message," what is the best definition of the word relaying?
   a. telling
   b. passing on
   c. giving out
   d. taking back

6. List three details from the story.

yesterday, delay, relay, holiday, essay, bayonet, betrayal, sway, displayed, haystack, mayonnaise, payable, praying, away

Worksheet 9 — "ay" May and the Soldiers – Cloze Reading

Name: _____ Number: _____

"ay" May and the Soldiers – Cloze Reading

Directions: Fill in the blanks with the correct "ay" word. Words may be used more than once.

Yesterday was a __holiday__. May wanted to play at the bay. She had been counting down the days for this break from school. Her plans were met with a __delay__. She had an essay due the next day.

May was feeling betrayed by herself for putting it off. She wanted to play. Only she knew she had to work on her __essay__. She sat down to write. She heard noises outside. She looked out the window. She saw soldiers marching towards her house. They had __bayonets__ in their hands.

May didn't know what to do. She hid in a haystack in her backyard. May heard one of the soldiers __relaying__ a message. He was saying that they were looking for their lost dog, Jay. He'd run off from the base.

May walked to the street.

"I'll __relay__ your message," May said. "I hope you find your dog."

"Thank you," the soldiers said. "He's a lab. He likes to eat creamy __mayonnaise__."

Then they went __away__.

"Mayonnaise! That's bad for dogs to eat," May thought.

May went up and down her block. May relayed the message. Then she went back to her essay.

Word Bank

away	relaying	essay	delay
mayonnaise	bayonets	holiday	relay

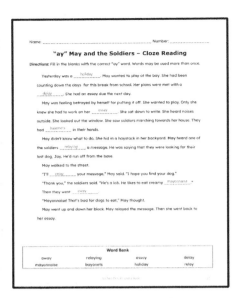

"ay" May and the Soldiers – Cloze Reading

"ay" All – Cloze Reading

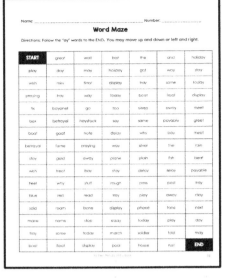

Word Maze

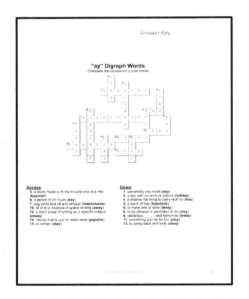

Answer Key — "ay" Digraph Words

Two Pencils and a Book

Phonics for Older Students

Long /ā/

Vowel Team
eigh, ey, ei, ea

Multi-Syllable
"eigh, ey, ei, and ea" Vowel Teams
Fluency Passages

Sentence Fluency: "eigh" – 1
Sentence Fluency: "eigh" – 2
Fluency: "eigh" – The Neighbor   Lexile Level 225L
Sentence Fluency: "ei"
Fluency: "ei" – The Reindeer   Lexile Level 300L
Sentence Fluency: "ey"
Fluency: "ey" – The Survey   Lexile Level 300L
Sentence Fluency: "ea"
Fluency 'ea: - Spring Break   Lexile Level 300L

Orthographic Mapping
How Does Orthographic Mapping Develop

When students are learning to read, they first start by sounding out each individual sound within a word. Over time, they begin to recognize the patterns they are reading because certain sounds appear over and over again in words. This resource is designed to provide such practice while reinforcing phonics.

This resource provides practice, so students recognize the patterns quickly without sounding them out every time.

A simple example of this is thinking about the word s*at*. Student see it so many times that they when they come across *rat* and *hat* and can read the *-at* part quickly because it has been orthographically mapped.

When students are introduced to new words, they use their sight word vocabulary to decode the new word because they have already created orthographic maps for these words.

Using the presentations for orthographic mapping and syllabication is easy - just follow this example by substituting the vowel team pattern you are working through.

1. Say the word *rap*. Have the student repeat it.

2. Ask them to say it again without the /r/. Be careful to say the sound /r/ and not the letter. The student should say *-ap*.

3. Ask them to say nap again, but this time instead of /r/ say /l/. The student should say *lap*.

4. Ask the student to say lap but add a /s/ to the beginning. The student should say *slap*.

Recognizing Which Long /a/
Interactive Notebook Page

Spelling Long /a/. Things to ask yourself.

Which Long /a/ Do I Use?

Is there more than one syllable?	"a_e" Examples: cake, same, behave	1 syllable words are very common
Is there a base word?	just "a" Examples table, acorn, baby	open syllables, can be one syllable but is usually two syllables
Where is the long a sound?	"ai" Examples: rain, sail, afraid	beginning or middle of a base word
Could a word be one of those rare long spellings (ey, ei, ea)?	"ay" Examples: play, say, away	end of one syllable word
	"ey", "eigh", "ei" they, sleight, beige, steak	very rare

Name: _____ Number: _____

Long /a/ Vowel Team "eigh"
Guided Worksheet

1. eight
2. weight
3. weighty
4. eighties
5. eighteen
6. neighbors
7. freight
8. sleigh
9. weightlifter
10. neighborly
11. height
12. neigh

Name: _____ Number: _____

Long /a/ Vowel Team "ei"
Guided Worksheet

1. vein
2. hey
3. veil
4. reindeer
5. beige
6. reign

Long /a/ Vowel Team "ey"
Guided Worksheet

1. disobey
2. prey
3. obey
4. convey
5. survey
6. they

Name: _____ Number: _____

Long /a/ Vowel Team "ea"
Guided Worksheet

1. break
2. breakout
3. breakdown
4. breaker
5. steak
6. great
7. greatness
8. greater

Name: _____ Number: _____

Long /a/ Vowel Team eigh, ey, ei, ea
Guided Worksheet

eight	vein
weight	hey
weighty	disobey
eighties	prey
eighteen	obey
neighbors	convey
freight	survey
sleigh	they
weightlifter	
neighborly	break
height	breakout
neigh	breakdown
	breaker
veil	steak
reindeer	great
beige	greatness
reign	greater

Pacing Guide For This Section

I move through a presentation per day in the following order:

'ei Presentation'

'eigh' Presentation

'ey' Presentation

'ea' Presentation

Option 1:

Day 1:
- Move through eigh presentation
- Practice "fluency" with Sentence Fluency 1
- Move through other Fluency "The Neighbor" and exercises.

Day 2:
- Review the previous day's vowel team- eigh.
- Do a final timed fluency read of the passage of "The Neighbor."
- Guide through "ei"
- Work through "ei" activities beginning with sentence fluency.

Day 3:
- Review the previous day's vowel team – "ei"
- Do a final timed fluency read of the passage of "The Reindeer"
- Guide through "ey"
- Walk through "ey activities beginning with sentence fluency.

Day 4:
- Review the previous day's vowel team – "ey"
- Do a final timed fluency read of the passage of "The Survey"
- Guide through "ea"
- Work through "ea" activities beginning with sentence fluency.

Option 2:

Divide each vowel team into two days.
- A DAYs– Presentations plus sentence fluency and interactive workbook pages
- B DAYs - Review vowel team – do fluency passage, comprehension and exercises

Name: _____ Number: _____

Test Date 1: _____ Test Date 2: _____

Long /a/ Vowel Team eigh, ey, ei, ea
Teacher Page

Teacher Say: Put your finger on the first word. We are going to read down the column. Read each word. Begin.

Word	Correct	Word	Correct
eight		vein	
weight		hey	
weighty		disobey	
eighties		prey	
eighteen		obey	
neighbors		convey	
freight		survey	
sleigh		they	
weightlifter			
neighborly		break	
height		breakout	
neigh		breakdown	
		breaker	
veil		steak	
reindeer		great	
beige		greatness	
reign		greater	

Name: _____ Number: _____

Test Date 1: _____ Test Date 2: _____

Long /a/ Vowel Team eigh, ey, ei, ea
Student Page

Word	Word
eight	vein
weight	hey
weighty	disobey
eighties	prey
eighteen	obey
neighbors	convey
freight	survey
sleigh	they
weightlifter	
neighborly	break
height	breakout
neigh	breakdown
	breaker
veil	steak
reindeer	great
beige	greatness
reign	greater

Phonics for Older Students

Long /ā/

Vowel Team
'eigh'

"eigh" Vowel Team - Interactive Notebook Page

Paste small rectangle into notebook to make a flap.

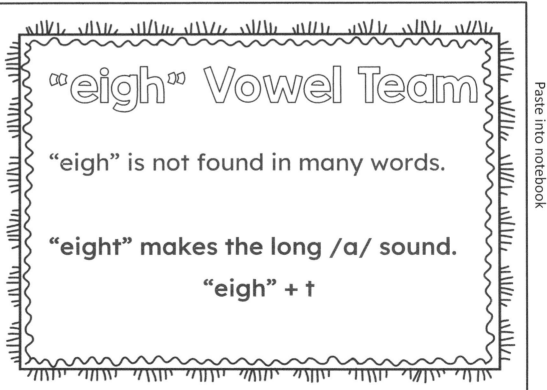

Paste into notebook

Name: _____ Number: _____

Word Pocket

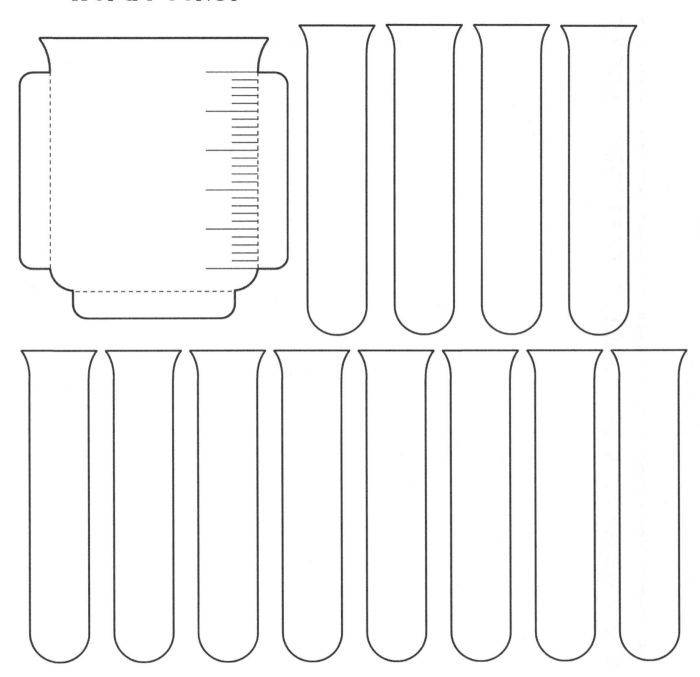

Write one "eigh" word per beaker: eight, weight, weighty, eighties, eighteen, neighbors, freight, sleigh, weightlifter, neighborly height, neigh

eight, EIGHTIES, EIGHTEEN, height, FREIGHT, sleigh, eight, EIGHTIES, EIGHTEEN, height, FREIGHT, sleigh eight, EIGHTIES, EIGHTEEN, height, FREIGHT, sleigh weight, weighty,

neighbors, neigh,

neighborly,

weightlifter

weight, weighty,

neighbors, neigh,

neighborly,

weightlifter

Sentence Fluency: "eigh" – Passage 17

The neighbors are having a party.	06
The neighbors are eating at eight.	12
We are going to eat at the neighbors.	20
We are going to eat at the neighbors at eight.	30
It is an eighties party.	35
The neighbors are having an eighties party.	42
We are going to eat at eight at the neighbors.	52
The neighbors are having an eighties party.	59
We'll eat at the eighties party.	65
It was neighborly for them to ask us to the party.	76
It is a weighty task to have a party.	85
They are having two contests.	90
They are having two contests at the party.	98
We have to guess the weight of a bag of eighties shoes.	110
We have to guess the height of a stack of books.	121
The eighties party will be great!	127

Words Read: _____	Words Read: _____	Words Read: _____
minus mistakes: _____	minus mistakes: _____	minus mistakes: _____
equals wpms: _____	equals wpms: _____	equals wpms: _____

Name: _____ Number: _____

Sentence Fluency: "eigh" – Passage 18

We eat at eight.	04
How much to you weigh?	09
What is your weight?	13
How tall are you?	17
What is your height?	21
When will you be eighteen?	26
Did you see the train?	31
It was a freight train.	36
It was a long freight train.	42
The freight train left at eight.	48
Those are my neighbors.	52
They live next door.	56
It is snowing.	59
Get out the sleigh.	63
We will get out the sleigh for the snow.	72
We will give our neighbors a ride.	79
We will give our neighbors a ride on the sleigh.	89
It is the neighborly thing to do.	96

Words Read: _____	Words Read: _____	Words Read: _____
minus mistakes: _____	minus mistakes: _____	minus mistakes: _____
equals wpms: _____	equals wpms: _____	equals wpms: _____

Fluency: "eigh" – 225L – The Neighbor – Passage 19

My neighbor has a sleigh. He uses the sleigh in winter. My neighbor pulls	14
the sleigh. He pulls the sleigh with his horse.	23
The sleigh is cool. It is from the 1700s. It used to pull freight. The sleigh	39
used to pull freight. It was freight sleigh.	47
Today, my neighbor loads it with hay. He gives us all rides. Eight people fit	62
in the front of the sleigh. Eighteen fit in the back.	73
We love the sleigh rides.	78
My neighbor has four horses. They pull the sleigh.	87
"Neigh," the horses say. Then they are off.	95
The horses are 15 hands high. They are pretty tall. Each horse weighs 1000	109
pounds. They are big horses.	114
The horses have a weighty task. They have a weighty task of pulling the	128
sleigh.	129
My neighbor is the best.	134
My neighbor's sleigh rides are the best.	141
I live in the best neighborhood in the world.	150

Words Read: _____	Words Read: _____	Words Read: _____
minus mistakes: _____	minus mistakes: _____	minus mistakes: _____
equals wpms: _____	equals wpms: _____	equals wpms: _____

Fluency Comprehension: "eigh" The Neighbor

Directions: Please select the best response.

1. How many neighbors ride in the back of the sleigh?

    a. eight

    b. eighteen

    c. eighty

    d. eighty-eight

2. What is a weighty task?

    a. being a neighbor

    b. loading hay

    c. giving sleigh rides

    d. pulling the sleigh

3. Read first paragraph. What is the best definition for the word <u>sleigh</u>?

    a. train

    b. car

    c. truck

    d. sled

4. What is the reading mostly about?

    a. a train gives hayrides

    b. a neighbor with a sleigh

    c. a neighbor with a sleigh hauls freight

    d. a neighbor with a sleigh gives sleigh rides

The vowels "eigh" makes the long /a/ sound in words like freight, sleigh, eight, and neighbor.

Underline the "eigh" vowel team in the words below.

Write rain tjree times. Underline the vowel team.
_____ _____ _____

Write sleigh three times. Underline the vowel team.
_____ _____ _____

Write eight three times. Underline the vowel team.
_____ _____ _____

Write neighbor three times. Underline the vowel team.
_____ _____ _____

Name: _____ Number: _____

"eigh" The Neighbor – Cloze Reading

Directions: Fill in the blanks with the correct "eigh" word. Words may be used more than once.

"My neighbor has a sleigh. He uses the sleigh in winter. My _____ pulls the

sleigh. He pulls the _____ with his horse.

The sleigh is cool. It is from the 1700s. It used to pull freight. The sleigh used to pull

_____. It was freight sleigh.

Today, my neighbor loads it with hay. He gives us all rides. Eight people fit in the front

of the sleigh. Eighteen fit in the back. That's _____ in the front. That's

_____more in the back. That's a lot of people.

We love the sleigh rides.

My _____ has four horses. They pull the sleigh.

"Neigh," the horses say. Then they are off.

The horses are 15 hands high. They are pretty tall. Each horse _____ 1000

pounds. They are big horses.

The horses have a weighty task. They have a _____ task of pulling the

_____.

My neighbor is the best.

My _____ sleigh rides are the best.

I live in the best neighborhood in the world.

Word Bank				
eighteen	neighbor	freight	sleigh	neighbor's
eight	weighs	weighty	neighbor	sleigh

Name: _____ Number: _____

'eigh' Long A Word Search

Directions: Find the "eigh" words. The words can be up or down, left to right, or diagonal.

```
E  I  G  H  T  I  E  S  O  N  F  R  E  I  G  H  T  H
I  T  H  I  N  G  L  P  O  V  I  W  E  I  G  H  T  E
G  E  S  T  M  I  N  E  O  L  N  E  K  N  G  U  O  V
H  L  N  L  P  O  E  I  G  H  T  I  E  S  P  N  C  L
T  H  R  I  E  N  B  G  O  I  N  G  U  E  S  E  T  M
E  S  T  E  R  I  N  H  L  I  H  H  P  I  T  I  A  S
E  N  G  L  I  N  G  T  A  L  Y  L  Y  O  U  G  H  E
N  E  I  E  H  T  E  H  N  N  E  I  G  H  C  H  X  U
W  O  W  E  I  G  H  T  Y  E  S  F  A  C  T  B  O  I
O  W  K  I  E  G  I  N  Z  C  L  T  I  L  N  O  I  K
Z  L  N  E  I  G  H  B  O  R  I  E  M  R  Z  R  M  L
X  O  H  E  I  G  H  T  H  E  I  R  O  L  M  L  D  I
T  H  E  R  E  I  N  O  M  O  D  O  I  M  X  Y  W  K
E  I  G  H  T  E  E  N  P  A  N  E  I  G  H  B  O  R
```

Word Bank					
eight	weight	weighty	eighties	eighteen	neighbor
sleigh	weightlifter	neighborly	height	neigh	freight

Name: _____ Number: _____

'eigh' Long A Word Maze

Directions: Follow the "eigh" words to the END. **You may move up and down or left and right.**

START	rain	main	play	day	may	pay
eight	bay	faithful	way	ray	say	clay
eighty	pray	rainy	display	sleep	agree	guarantee
eighteen	aim	maintain	today	display	array	today
eighties	neighbor	delay	relay	holiday	essay	betrayal
pain	neighbors	haystack	way	employee	steep	queen
waiting	freight	domain	afraid	pray	saying	display
breeze	sleigh	weight	neigh	height	weight	breed
feed	horse	house	sail	zookeeper	weighty	employee
degree	spray	guarantee	draining	exclaim	height	peaceful
feature	trainee	teenager	clean	frail	eighty	decrease
reason	zookeeper	eighties	freight	eighty	eight	tree
feel	sleepover	neigh	reason	attain	teach	creature
theater	queen	weight	degree	paint	contain	waitress
beaver	freeze	sleigh	cheer	beneath	beach	rain
beat	meat	neighbor	neighborly	freight	eight	END

Phonics for Older Students

Long /ā/

Vowel Team
'ei'

Name: _____ Number: _____

"ei" Vowel Team - Interactive Notebook Page

"ei" Words

veil
reindeer
beige
reign
vein

"ei" Vowel Team

"ei" is not found in many words.

"vein" makes the long /a/ sound.

Name: _____ Number: _____

Word Pocket

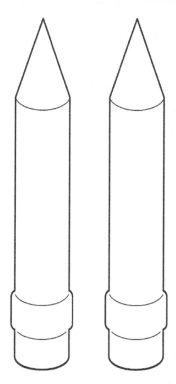

Write one "ei" Word on each pencil – veil, reindeer, beige, reign, vein

veil
reindeer
beige
reign
vein

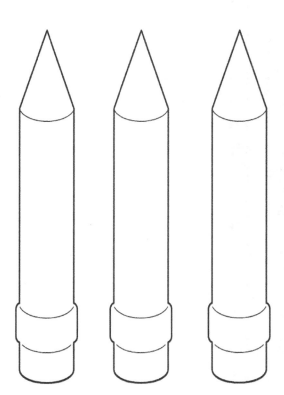

veil, reindeer, beige,
reign, vein

veil, reindeer, beige,
reign, vein

veil, reindeer, beige,
reign, vein

veil, reindeer, beige,
reign, vein

Name: _____ Number: _____

Sentence Fluency: "ei" – Passage 20

The blood ran through is veins.	06
The blood ran through the reindeer's veins.	13
The reindeer had beige fur.	18
The fur of the reindeer was beige.	25
Jake had a beige coat.	30
Jake wore his beige coat riding	36
Jake wore his beige coat riding reindeer.	43
Seema wore a hat with a veil.	50
The hat and veil were beige.	55
The beige veil covered Seema's face.	61
Hey! There goes the reigning queen!	67
Hey! There goes the reigning queen riding a reindeer.	76
There goes the queen in a beige hat.	84
There goes the queen in a beige hat with a veil.	95
The queen in the beige hat is riding a reindeer.	105

Words Read: _____	Words Read: _____	Words Read: _____
minus mistakes: _____	minus mistakes: _____	minus mistakes: _____
equals wpms: _____	equals wpms: _____	equals wpms: _____

Fluency: "ei" – 300L – The Reindeer – Passage 21

The sun was high in the sky. The reindeer were playing in the field. They	14
were jumping over logs. They were excited. It was a beautiful day. Plus, the	28
reigning queen was coming.	32
The queen had reigned over the reindeer for forty years. Her reign had	45
been a good one for the reindeer. The queen had built the reindeer a	49
beautiful barn. She fed them well. She hired people to brush their coats.	72
The reindeer's coats were beautiful. They were beige. They were a creamy	84
beige. Their creamy beige coats looked like coffee with milk. They were	96
lovely.	98
"Hey," Robbie reindeer called. "Here comes the queen."	106
"I love the reigning queen's new hat!" Rita reindeer said. "It has a veil."	120
"The veil barely covers her face. And the color is great. It's beige like our	135
coats," Robbie said.	138
"A veil for riding reindeer? The reigning queen has never worn a veil to ride	153
reindeer," Rita said.	156
The queen overheard them "Today is a special day. We are all riding in a	170
parade. It is the 40th birthday of my reign."	179
The reindeer were excited. They fluffed their beige coats. They were ready	191
to go.	193

Words Read: _____	Words Read: _____	Words Read: _____
minus mistakes: _____	minus mistakes: _____	minus mistakes: _____
equals wpms: _____	equals wpms: _____	equals wpms: _____

Fluency Comprehension: "ei" The Reindeer

Directions: Please select the best response.

1. What color was the queen's had?

   a. coffee

   b. cream

   c. brown

   d. beige

2. What had the reigning queen never worn to ride?

   a. a hat

   b. a beige coat

   c. a beige veil

   d. a beige hat

3. In the passage, what is the best definition for the word <u>reign</u>?

   a. water that fall from the sky

   b. a royal office held by a queen or king

   c. an elected office held by a king or queen

   d. a group of reindeer

4. What is the reading mostly about?

   a. a reigning queen feeds her reindeer

   b. a queen rides her reindeer

   c. the reindeer get ready to ride in a parade for the queen

   d. a queen' forty-year reign

The vowels "ei" makes the long /a/ sound in words like beige, reign, veil, and reindeer.

Underline the "ei" vowel team in the words below.

Write beige three times. Underline the vowel team.

_____   _____   _____

Write reign three times. Underline the vowel team.

_____   _____   _____

Write veil three times. Underline the vowel team.

_____   _____   _____

Write reindeer three times. Underline the vowel team.

_____   _____   _____

Name: _____ Number: _____

"ei" The Reindeer – Cloze Reading

Directions: Fill in the blanks with the correct "ei" word. Words may be used more than once.

The sun was high in the sky. The reindeer were playing in the field. They were jumping over logs. They _____ were excited. It was a beautiful day. Plus, the reigning queen was coming.

The queen had _____ over the reindeer for forty years. Her reign had been a good one for the reindeer. The queen had built the _____a beautiful barn. She fed them well. She hired people to brush their coats.

The reindeer's coats were beautiful. They were _____. They were a creamy beige. Their creamy beige coats looked like coffee with milk. They were lovely.

"Hey," Robbie _____ called. "Here comes the queen."

"I love the reigning queen's new hat!" Rita reindeer said. "It has a _____."

"The veil barely covers her face. And the color is great. It's _____ like our coats," Robbie said.

"A veil for riding _____? The reigning queen has never worn a veil to ride reindeer," Rita said.

The queen overheard them "Today is a special day. We are all riding in a parade. It is the 40th birthday of my _____."

The reindeer were excited. They fluffed their beige coats. They were ready to go.

Word Bank			
reigned	reindeer	reign	reindeer
veil	beige	reindeer	beige

Name: _____ Number: _____

Long A - 'ei' - Word Maze

Directions: Follow the "ei" words to the END. You may move up and down or left and right.

START	veil	reindeer	play	day	may	pay
eight	bay	beige	reign	vein	veil	clay
eighty	pray	rainy	display	sleep	reindeer	guarantee
eighteen	aim	maintain	today	display	beige	today
eighties	neighbor	delay	veil	reindeer	reign	betrayal
pain	neighbors	haystack	way	employee	vein	queen
waiting	freight	domain	afraid	pray	veil	reindeer
breeze	sleigh	weight	neigh	height	weight	beige
feed	reign	vein	veil	reindeer	vein	reign
degree	reign	guarantee	vein	exclaim	height	peaceful
feature	trainee	teenager	reign	frail	eighty	decrease
reason	zookeeper	eighties	reindeer	eighty	eight	tree
feel	sleepover	neigh	reign	beige	reindeer	beige
theater	queen	weight	degree	paint	contain	reign
beaver	freeze	sleigh	cheer	beneath	beach	vein
beat	meat	neighbor	neighborly	freight	eight	END

Phonics for Older Students

Long /ā/

Vowel Team 'ey'

Two Pencils and a Book

Name: _____ Number: _____

Words to Sentences

Directions: Unscramble the sentences.

1. were in the The reindeer barn.   _____

_____

2. coats The had beige reindeer.   _____

_____

3. had a long queen reign The .   _____

_____

4. a beige The had veil hat.   _____

_____

5. vampire's through Blood ran the cold veins.   _____

_____

Definitions.
1. <u>reindeer:</u> a species of deer native to the Arctic.
2. <u>beige:</u> a pale sandy yellowish-brown color.
3. <u>reign:</u> to hold a royal office.
4. <u>veil:</u> material worn to cover one's face.
5. <u>veins</u> the body's way to carry blood back to the heart.

"ey" Vowel Team - Interactive Notebook Page

Vowel Team
"ey"

"ey" Vowel Team

ey" is not found in many words.

"ey" makes the long /a/ sound like in the word "they."

Word Pocket

Cut out the shapes. Fold the tabs on the pot at the dotted lines. Paste to your notebook. Write one "ey" Word on each flower – hey, disobey, prey, obey convey, survey, they.

hey, disobey,

prey, obey,

convey, survey,

they, hey,

disobey, prey,

obey, convey,

survey, they

Sentence Fluency: "ey" – Passage 22

We have to obey the rules of the game.	09
If we don't obey the rules, we can't play.	18
Disobey the rules and get a foul.	25
I hope you don't disobey the rules.	32
We need you on the team.	38
We need you on the team, so obey the rules.	48
Convey means to move from place to place.	56
Convey the balls to the game.	62
Convey the basketball to the game.	68
Hey, those balls are flat.	73
Don't convey the flat balls.	78
Bring the good balls and obey the rules.	86
Hey! How did the balls get flat?	93
Survey the players.	96
Survey the player to see who can play.	104
Survey the players who can be at the game.	113
And make sure they follow all of the rules.	122

Words Read: _____	Words Read: _____	Words Read: _____
minus mistakes: _____	minus mistakes: _____	minus mistakes: _____
equals wpms: _____	equals wpms: _____	equals wpms: _____

Fluency: "ey" – 300L – The Survey – Passage 23

Lucas and Mike were doing a project for math. They were taking a survey.	14
The survey was for rules. The survey was for how many rules were obeyed.	28
They knew most school rules were obeyed. They also knew some were	40
disobeyed. They were going to survey their friends.	48
"Hey!" Lucas yelled. "Hey, Mike. Did you bring the survey?"	58
"Yes, here's the survey," Mike said.	64
"You take the field. I'll take the gym," Lucas said. "I hope our friends tell	79
the truth."	81
"I know. What if they don't say they broke the rules? What if they don't	96
say they disobey?"	99
"Then they'll fall prey to me!"	105
"And what does that mean," Lucas asked.	112
"They won't get any of my mom's cookies," Mike said.	122
"And you mom makes the best cookies," Lucas said. "They don't want to	135
fall prey to that."	139
"They don't have to give their names," Lucas said. "We have to convey this	153
to them. We have to convey that we won't use their names."	165
The boys set out to survey their friends.	173
It took all lunch to do. The finished as the bell rang.	185
"I think we did okay," Mike said.	192
"People said they obeyed the rules. People also said they disobeyed the	204
rules. Let's go tally the results."	210
They turned in their survey. They turned in their math project. They got an	224
A.	225

Words Read: _____	Words Read: _____	Words Read: _____
minus mistakes: _____	minus mistakes: _____	minus mistakes: _____
equals wpms: _____	equals wpms: _____	equals wpms: _____

Fluency Comprehension: "ey" The Survey

Directions: Please select the best response.

1. What was point of survey for?
   a. a math project about school
   b. fixing the gym
   c. a math project about obeying the rules
   d. a math project for a new gym

2. What is the best synonym for the word convey?
   a. suggest
   b. carry to take
   c. pass on or move on
   d. take back

3. In the passage, what is the best definition for the word disobey?
   a. break the rules
   b. follow the rules
   c. know the rules
   d. survey the rules

4. What is the reading mostly about?
   a. taking a survey
   b. finishing a survey
   c. taking a survey about following the rules
   d. getting an a on a survey

The vowels "ey" makes the long /a/ sound in words like survey, obey, disobey, and convey.

Underline the "ey" vowel team in the words below.

| Write survey three times. Underline the vowel team. |
| _____   _____   _____ |

| Write obey three times. Underline the vowel team. |
| _____   _____   _____ |

| Write disobey three times. Underline the vowel team. |
| _____   _____   _____ |

| Write convey three times. Underline the vowel team. |
| _____   _____   _____ |

"ey" The Survey – Cloze Reading

Directions: Fill in the blanks with the correct "ey" word. Words may be used more than once.

Lucas and Mike were doing a project for math. They were taking a survey. The survey was for rules. The survey was for how many rules were _____. They knew most school rules were obeyed. They also knew some were _____. They were going to _____ their friends.

"Hey!" Lucas yelled. "Hey, Mike. Did you bring the _____?"

"Yes, here's the survey," Mike said.

"You take the field. I'll take the gym," Lucas said. "I hope our friends tell the truth."

"I know. What if they don't say they broke the rules? What if they don't say they _____?"

"Then they'll fall prey to me!"

"And what does that mean," Lucas asked.

"If they fall _____ to me, They won't get any of my mom's cookies," Mike said.

"And you mom makes the best cookies," Lucas said. "_____ don't want to fall prey to that."

"_____ don't have to give their names," Lucas said. "We have to _____ this to them. We have to convey that we won't use their names."

The boys set out to _____ their friends.

It took all lunch to do. The finished as the bell rang.

Word Bank				
survey	disobeyed	disobeyed	prey	they
convey	survey	obeyed	survey	they

Name: _____ Number: _____

Long A 'ey' Word Maze

Directions: Follow the "ey" words to the END. You may move up and down or left and right.

START	veil	reindeer	play	day	may	pay
hey	bay	beige	reign	vein	veil	clay
disobey	pray	rainy	display	sleep	reindeer	guarantee
survey	aim	maintain	today	display	beige	today
prey	neighbor	delay	veil	reindeer	reign	betrayal
obey	neighbors	haystack	way	employee	vein	queen
they	freight	domain	afraid	pray	veil	reindeer
convey	hey	disobey	convey	obey	weight	beige
feed	reign	vein	veil	survey	vein	reign
degree	reign	guarantee	vein	hey	height	peaceful
feature	obey	convey	prey	disobey	eighty	decrease
reason	prey	eighties	reindeer	eighty	eight	tree
feel	hey	neigh	reign	beige	reindeer	beige
theater	disobey	convey	degree	paint	contain	reign
beaver	obey	they	covey	prey	hey	survey
beat	meat	neighbor	neighborly	freight	eight	END

Phonics for Older Students

Long /ā/

Vowel Team 'ea'

Name: _____ Number: _____

"ea" Vowel Team - Interactive Notebook Page

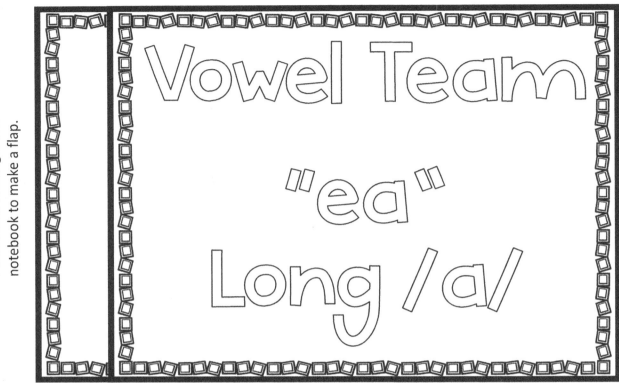

Vowel Team "ea" Long /a/

"ea" Words

break
breakout
breakdown
steak
great
greatness
greater

"ea" Vowel Team

"ea" makes the long /a/ sound like in the word "break."

Name: _____ Number: _____

Word Pocket

Cut out the shapes. Fold the tabs on the pot at the dotted lines. Paste to your notebook. Write one "ea" word on each stem: Break, breakout, breakdown, breaker, steak, great, greatness, greater.

Two Pencils and a Book

BREAK, breakout, steak, BREAKDOWN, great, breaker, GREATNESS, greater

Sentence Fluency: "ea" - Passage 24

It is time for a break.	06
It is time for a break from school.	14
If the students don't get a break, they'll breakout.	23
They will breakdown before they breakout.	29
If they don't get a break, they will breakdown, and then they will breakout.	43
Over break I'm going to see a breaker.	51
A breaker is a sea wave.	57
A breaker is a sea wave that breaks into foam.	67
We ate steaks on the beach.	73
We ate steaks on the beach watching the breakers.	82
It was great.	85
It was great to watch the breakers.	92
It was great to eat steaks.	98
It was even greater to eat steaks and watch the breakers at the same time.	113

Words Read: _____	Words Read: _____	Words Read: _____
minus mistakes: _____	minus mistakes: _____	minus mistakes: _____
equals wpms: _____	equals wpms: _____	equals wpms: _____

Fluency: "ea" – 300L – Spring Break – Passage 25

Emma and Marie are going to the beach. They are going to the beach for	15
spring break.	17
"One more week," Marie said. "I can't wait. It is going to be great."	31
"The greatest!" Emma said. "We can swim. We can surf. We can drink fruity	45
drinks. We can bask in the sun. I love the ocean."	56
"We have to be careful of the breakers. They hit pretty hard," Marie said.	70
"I bet they are big. The North Shore is the greatest. It is known for its	86
breakers."	87
"In all of its greatness, it can't beat Butlers," Emma said. Butlers was a	101
steakhouse. Butlers made the best steaks in the world. The girls couldn't wait	114
to eat steak at Butlers. "The breakers are great. Butlers is the greatest."	127
"Yum! And the best part is the ocean. We can see the breakers from	141
Butlers."	142
"I think the best part is the steak," Emma said.	152
"Steak and breakers. Both are great! I can't wait!"	161

Words Read: _____	Words Read: _____	Words Read: _____
minus mistakes: _____	minus mistakes: _____	minus mistakes: _____
equals wpms: _____	equals wpms: _____	equals wpms: _____

Name: _____ Number: _____

Fluency Comprehension: "ea" Spring Break

Directions: Please select the best response.

1. Emma and Marie were going to
   a.   make steak
   b.   make the greatest steak
   c.   ride the breakers
   d.   go to the beach

2. What is the best synonym for the word <u>breaker</u>?
   a.   surf
   b.   shore
   c.   sand
   d.   ocean

3. In the passage, what is the best definition for the word <u>greatness</u>?
   a.   something that is common
   b.   something that is awesome
   c.   something that is plain
   d.   something that is perfect

4. What is the reading mostly about?
   a.   two people eating steak
   b.   two people watching breakers
   c.   two people going to the beach
   d.   two people talking about what they are going to do over spring break

---

The vowels "ea" makes the long /a/ sound in words like break, great, steak, and breakout.

Underline the "ea" vowel team in the words below.

Write break times. Underline the vowel team.
_____ _____ _____

Write great three times. Underline the vowel team.
_____ _____ _____

Write steak three times. Underline the vowel team.
_____ _____ _____

Write breakout three times. Underline the vowel team.
_____ _____ _____

"ea" Spring Break – Cloze Reading

Directions: Fill in the blanks with the correct "ea" word. Words may be used more than once.

Emma and Marie are going to the beach. They are going to the beach for spring

break.

"One more week until _____," Marie said. "I can't wait. It is going to be

great."

"The _____!" Emma said. "We can swim. We can surf. We can drink fruity

drinks. We can bask in the sun. I love the ocean."

"We have to be careful of the _____. They hit pretty hard," Marie said.

"I bet they are big. The North Shore is the greatest. It is known for its breakers."

"In all of its _____, it can't beat Butlers," Emma said. Butlers was a

steakhouse. Butlers made the best _____ in the world. The girls couldn't wait to

eat steak at Butlers. "The breakers are great. Butlers is the _____."

"Yum! And the best part is the ocean. We can see the _____ from Butlers."

"I think the best part is the _____," Emma said.

"Steak and breakers. Both are great! I can't wait!"

Word Bank				
steaks	greatest	breakers	greatness	steaks
	greatest	breakers	break	

Name: _____ Number: _____

Long A -ea' Word Maze

Directions: Follow the "ea" words to the END. You may move up and down or left and right.

START	veil	reindeer	play	day	may	pay
break	bay	beige	reign	vein	veil	clay
breakout	break	great	greater	steak	reindeer	guarantee
breakdown	break	great	greatest	greatness	greats	today
breaker	neighbor	delay	veil	reindeer	reign	betrayal
steak	neighbors	haystack	way	employee	vein	queen
great	freight	domain	afraid	pray	veil	reindeer
greatness	greater	break	breakout	steak	weight	beige
feed	reign	break	veil	break	vein	reign
degree	reign	breakout	vein	breakout	height	peaceful
feature	obey	breakdown	prey	breakdown	eighty	decrease
reason	prey	breaker	reindeer	breaker	eight	tree
feel	hey	steak	reign	steak	reindeer	beige
theater	disobey	break	degree	great	contain	reign
beaver	obey	they	covey	break	hey	survey
beat	meat	neighbor	neighborly	steak	breakdown	END

Words to Sentences

Directions: Unscramble the sentences.

1. The were waves great.   _____

_____

2. hit breakers beach The the.   _____

_____

3. was the Spring break greatest.   _____

_____

4. We ate break over steak.   _____

_____

5. breakdown We the problem will.   _____

_____

Write two connected sentences using the words: break, steak, greater, and greatest.

_____

_____

_____

_____

Word Search - ey, ei, and ea

Directions: Find the "ey, ei, and ea" vowel team words. The words can be up or down, left to right, or diagonal.

```
V  E  I  L  T  H  E  R  D  I  S  O  B  E  Y  A  I  B
N  P  I  E  T  S  U  R  V  E  Y  I  M  N  A  B  T  R
R  U  R  A  L  T  R  C  O  N  V  E  Y  I  C  R  I  E
V  E  I  N  O  O  B  E  Y  E  D  E  E  R  O  E  O  A
C  N  I  N  K  E  B  R  E  A  K  B  R  E  M  A  G  K
N  E  A  N  I  O  I  G  R  E  A  T  P  O  M  K  R  O
A  E  T  E  D  E  O  U  T  B  R  E  A  K  A  D  E  U
G  R  H  S  R  E  I  G  N  O  T  H  I  N  G  O  A  T
O  B  E  Y  E  R  E  N  O  U  G  T  I  H  I  W  T  H
E  L  Y  L  O  W  O  R  W  Z  O  M  O  I  T  N  E  P
A  I  B  P  S  R  B  R  E  A  K  E  R  Q  O  T  R  E
B  T  R  R  Y  E  R  E  I  G  N  I  N  G  U  G  R  R
S  R  H  E  Y  O  T  G  R  E  A  T  N  E  S  S  O  T
Y  E  F  Y  A  U  G  U  E  L  I  B  E  I  G  E  U  G
```

Word Bank

veil	reindeer	beige	reign	vein	hey
disobey	prey	obey	convey	survey	they
break	breakout	breakdown	breaker	great	greatness
	greater	outbreak	reigning	obeyed	

Panel 1 — Fluency Comprehension: "eigh" The Neighbor

Name: _____ Number: _____

Fluency Comprehension: "eigh" The Neighbor

Directions: Please select the best response.

1. How many neighbors ride in the back of the sleigh?
   a. eight
   b. eighteen
   c. eighty
   d. eighty-eight

2. What is a weighty task?
   a. being a neighbor
   b. loading hay
   c. giving sleigh rides
   d. pulling the sleigh

3. Read first paragraph. What is the best definition for the word sleigh?
   a. train
   b. car
   c. truck
   d. sled

4. What is the reading mostly about?
   a. a train gives hayrides
   b. a neighbor with a sleigh
   c. a neighbor with a sleigh hauls freight
   d. a neighbor with a sleigh gives sleigh rides

The vowels "eigh" makes the long /a/ sound in words like freight, sleigh, eight, and neighbor.

Underline the "eigh" vowel team in the words below.

Write rain freight times. Underline the vowel team.
_____   _____

Write sleigh three times. Underline the vowel team.

Write eight three times. Underline the vowel team.

Write neighbor three times. Underline the vowel team.

Panel 2 — "eigh" The Neighbor – Cloze Reading

Name: _____ Number: _____

"eigh" The Neighbor – Cloze Reading

Directions: Fill in the blanks with the correct "eigh" word. Words may be used more than once.

"My neighbor has a sleigh. He uses the sleigh in winter. My _____ pulls the sleigh. He pulls the _____ with his horse.

The sleigh is cool. It is from the 1700s. It used to pull freight. The sleigh used to pull _____. It was freight sleigh.

Today, my neighbor loads it with hay. He gives us all rides. Eight people fit in the front of the sleigh. Eighteen fit in the back. That's _____ in the front. That's _____ more in the back. That's a lot of people.

We love the sleigh rides.

My _____ has four horses. They pull the sleigh.

"Neigh," the horses say. Then they are off.

The horses are 15 hands high. They are pretty tall. Each horse _____ 1000 pounds. They are big horses.

The horses have a weighty task. They have a _____ task of pulling the _____.

My neighbor is the best.

My _____ sleigh rides are the best.

I live in the best neighborhood in the world.

Word Bank					
eighteen	neighbor	freight	sleigh	neighbor's	
eight	weighs	weighty	neighbor	sleigh	

Panel 3 — Word Search

Name: _____ Number: _____

Word Search

Directions: Find the "eigh" words. The words can be up or down, left to right, or diagonal.

E I G H T I E S   F R E I G H T
I   W E I G H T
G S   E   E
H   L   E I G H T I E S N   G
T   E   G G   E G   I   E
E   I   H   H   I H   I
N E   G T   L   G   N E I G H
    W E I G H T Y   F   H B
    G   T   O
N E I G H B O R E   R   L
H E I G H T   R   L   Y
E I G H T E E N   N E I G H B O R

Word Bank					
eight	weight	weighty	eighties	eighteen	neighbor
sleigh	weightlifter	neighborly	height	neigh	freight

Panel 4 — Word Maze ("eigh")

Name: _____ Number: _____

Word Maze

Directions: Follow the "eigh" words to the END. You may move up and down or left and right.

START	rain	main	clay	day	may	pay
eight	bay	faithful	way	ray	ray	clay
eighty	gray	rainy	display	sleep	agree	guarantee
eighteen	aim	maintain	today	display	array	today
eighties	neighbor	delay	relay	holiday	essay	betrayal
rain	neighbors	haystack	way	employee	steep	queen
waiting	freight	domain	afraid	array	saying	display
breeze	sleigh	weight	neigh	height	weight	breed
feed	horse	house	sail	zookeeper	weighty	employee
degree	spray	guarantee	draining	exclaim	height	peaceful
feature	trainee	teenager	clean	frail	eighty	decrease
reason	zookeeper	eighties	freight	eighty	eight	free
feel	sleepover	neigh	reason	attain	teach	creature
theater	queen	weight	degree	paint	contain	waitress
beaver	freeze	sleigh	cheer	beneath	breach	rain
beat	meat	neighbor	neighborly	freight	eight	END

Panel 5 — Fluency Comprehension: "ei" The Reindeer

Name: _____ Number: _____

Fluency Comprehension: "ei" The Reindeer

Directions: Please select the best response.

1. What color was the queen's hat?
   a. coffee
   b. cream
   c. brown
   d. beige

2. What had the reigning queen never worn to ride?
   a. a hat
   b. a beige coat
   c. a beige veil
   d. a beige hat

3. In the passage, what is the best definition for the word reign?
   a. water that fall from the sky
   b. a royal office held by a queen or king
   c. an elected office held by a king or queen
   d. a group of reindeer

4. What is the reading mostly about?
   a. a reigning queen feeds her reindeer
   b. a queen rides her reindeer
   c. the reindeer get ready to ride in a parade for the queen
   d. a queen' forty-year reign

The vowels "ei" makes the long /a/ sound in words like beige, reign, veil, and reindeer.

Underline the "ei" vowel team in the words below.

Write beige times. Underline the vowel team.

Write reign three times. Underline the vowel team.

Write veil three times. Underline the vowel team.

Write reindeer three times. Underline the vowel team.

Panel 6 — "ei" The Reindeer – Cloze Reading

Name: _____ Number: _____

"ei" The Reindeer – Cloze Reading

Directions: Fill in the blanks with the correct "ei" word. Words may be used more than once.

The sun was high in the sky. The reindeer were playing in the field. They were jumping over logs. They _____ were excited. It was a beautiful day. Plus, the reigning queen was coming.

The queen had _____ over the reindeer for forty years. Her reign had been a good one for the reindeer. The queen had built the _____ a beautiful barn. She fed them well. She hired people to brush their coats.

The reindeer's coats were beautiful. They were _____. They were a creamy beige. Their creamy beige coats looked like coffee with milk. They were lovely.

"Hey," Robbie _____ called. "Here comes the queen."

"I love the reigning queen's new hat!" Rita reindeer said. "It has a _____."

"The veil barely covers her face. And the color is great. It's _____ like our coats," Robbie said.

"A veil for riding _____? The reigning queen has never worn a veil to ride reindeer," Rita said.

The queen overheard them "Today is a special day. We are all riding in a parade. It is the 40th birthday of my _____."

The reindeer were excited. They fluffed their beige coats. They were ready to go.

Word Bank			
reigned	reindeer	reign	reindeer
veil	beige	reindeer	beige

Panel 7 — Word Maze ("ei")

Name: _____ Number: _____

Word Maze

Directions: Follow the "ei" words to the END. You may move up and down or left and right.

START	veil	reindeer	play	day	may	pay
eight	bay	beige	reign	vein	veil	clay
eighty	gray	rainy	display	sleep	reindeer	guarantee
eighteen	aim	maintain	today	display	beige	today
eighties	neighbor	delay	veil	reindeer	reign	betrayal
rain	neighbors	haystack	way	employee	vein	queen
waiting	freight	domain	afraid	pray	veil	reindeer
breeze	sleigh	weight	neigh	height	weight	beige
feed	reign	vein	veil	reindeer	vein	reign
degree	guarantee	vein	vein	exclaim	height	peaceful
feature	trainee	teenager	reign	frail	eighty	decrease
reason	zookeeper	eighties	reindeer	eighty	eight	true
feel	sleepover	reign	reign	beige	reindeer	true
theater	queen	weight	degree	paint	contain	reign
beaver	freeze	sleigh	cheer	beneath	breach	vein
beat	meat	neighbor	neighborly	freight	eight	END

Panel 8 — Words to Sentences

Name: _____ Number: _____

Words to Sentences

Directions: Unscramble the sentences.

1. The reindeer were in the barn.
   _____

2. The reindeer had beige coats.
   _____

3. The queen had a long reign.
   _____

4. The hat had a beige veil.
   _____

5. Blood ran cold through the vampire's veins.
   _____

Definitions:
1. reindeer: a species of deer native to the Arctic
2. beige: a pale sandy yellowish-brown color.
3. reign: to hold a royal office.
4. veil: material worn to cover one's face.
5. vein: the body's way to carry blood back to the heart.

Panel 9 — Fluency Comprehension: "ey" The Survey

Name: _____ Number: _____

Fluency Comprehension: "ey" The Survey

Directions: Please select the best response.

1. What was point of survey for?
   a. a math project about school
   b. fixing the gym
   c. a math project about obeying the rules
   d. a math project for a new gym

2. What is the best synonym for the word convey?
   a. suggest
   b. carry to take
   c. pass or move on
   d. take back

3. In the passage, what is the best definition for the word disobey?
   a. break the rules
   b. follow the rules
   c. know the rules
   d. survey the rules

4. What is the reading mostly about?
   a. taking a survey
   b. finishing a survey
   c. taking a survey about following the rules
   d. getting an on a on a survey

The vowels "ey" makes the long /a/ sound in words like survey, obey, disobey, and convey.

Underline the "ey" vowel team in the words below.

Write survey times. Underline the vowel team.

Write obey three times. Underline the vowel team.

Write disobey three times. Underline the vowel team.

Write convey three times. Underline the vowel team.

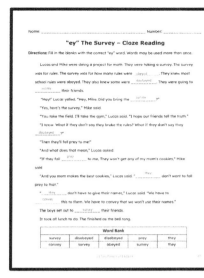

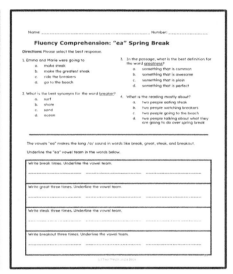
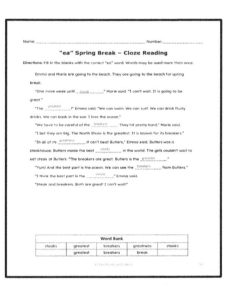

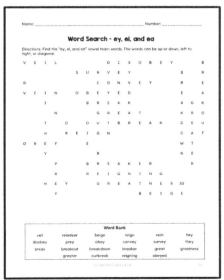

Two Pencils and a Book

ESCAPE ROOM GAME

Unlock the Long a Sound

Alice, of Wonderland fame, and Huckleberry Finn find themselves in Wonderland trying to save the English language.

The queen of hearts has taken all the words with the long a sound and locked them away. Help Alice and Huck solve the puzzles to find the keys to save English!

Puzzle Descriptions

<u>Scenario:</u> Huckleberry Finn follows Alice, of Wonderland fame, down the rabbit hole. It seems she was called back to Wonderland to save the day. The Queen of Hearts has locked all of the Long A words, in their various spelling forms, away in five boxes. It's up to Huck, Alice and your students to solve five puzzles that unlock different ways Long A is spelled and save the English language.

<u>Challenge 1:</u> "a_e" Alice and Huck find a note. They must find the key for the a_e box. To do so, they solve an a_e word search. There are various levels of this puzzle – one syllable words, two syllable, and multi-syllable all with and without word banks.

<u>Challenge 2:</u> "ai" Alice and Hunk run into the Mad Hatter and must solve a missing letter puzzle in order to unlock the "ai" words. There are two versions of this puzzle. One with some of the missing letters filled in and one without.

<u>Challenge 3:</u> "ay" Alice and Huck find Caterpillar – who has the note to find the key for the next box to unlock. They must solve a cryptogram.

<u>Challenge 4:</u> "eight" Huck and Alice meet Cheshire Cat and are tasked with solving a hidden message word search.

<u>Challenge 5:</u> Ways to Say Long A. Last, Alice and Huck must solve a logic puzzle to unlock the rest of the Long a words and must do so in time for tea.

<u>Challenge 6:</u> Assemble the keys for the secret message return from Wonderland.

This is a digital or print escape room challenge.

PRINT: How to Play.

1. Copy "Student Pages."

2. Divide students into pairs or groups. Tell students that they are responsible for reading the instructions and completing each assignment. Read:

   Alice, of Wonderland fame, and Huckleberry Finn have found themselves in Wonderland trying to save the English language.

   The queen of hearts has taken all the words with the long a sound and locked them away in five boxes. Help Alice and Huck solve the puzzles to find the keys to save English!

   Tell them that when they are finished with each puzzle, to bring their paper to the puzzle master and they will get a key and a word. In order to return from Wonderland, they'll need to assemble the words into a sentence.

3. **Option:** Make it a competition for accuracy and time, but don't allow groups to complete more than one puzzle at a time. If you distribute packets – this may occur. Tell students they will be disqualified for working on more than one puzzle at a time. Groups are also disqualified if they share answers with other groups. **Do not use this option if you feel it will in any way frustrate students.**

4. I do a debrief after the activity. What did students like? What was simple? What was difficult? What did they like best?

5. Google Slide link:

   https://docs.google.com/presentation/d/1xCo00ZGUDxTMWZiRhlLePdiJzj
   GYSJfGFxyO6sX3ghQ/edit?usp=sharing

Unlock the Long a Sound – Challenge Variations

Challenge 1:
Level 1: Students find four letter "a_e" words in a word search with a word bank.
Level 2. Students find four letter "a_e" words in a word search without a word bank.

- For Executive Function practice – Assign Level 1 with the Escape Room Assignment, then as a warm-up the day after, or a closer at the end of the day, assign Level 2.

Level 3: Students find five letter "a_e" words in a word search with a word bank.
Level 4: Students find five letter "a_e" words in a word search without a word bank.

- For Executive Function practice – Assign Level 3 with the Escape Room Assignment, then as a warm-up the day after, or a closer at the end of the day, assign Level 4.

Level 5: Students find multiple syllable "a_e" words in a word search with a word bank.
Level 6: Students find multiple syllable "a_e" words in a word search without a word bank.

- For Executive Function practice – Assign Level 5 with the Escape Room Assignment, then as a warm-up the day after, or a closer at the end of the day, assign Level 6.

Challenge 2 has two levels – one with some letters filled in. One completely blank.

Challenge 4 has two levels – one with some letters filled in. One completely blank.

Unlock the Long a Sound – Notes Page

Challenge 1:
Challenge 2:
Challenge 3:
Challenge 4:
Challenge 5:
Write the sentence here:

Name: _____

Unlock the Long a Sound

Huck Finn was in England. He saw Alice. You know. Alice of the Wonderland set. He saw her go down the hole. The hole was in the ground. He went after her.

"Who are you?" Alice asked. She looked around.

"I'm Hunk. I'm from the US. I'm here with my Aunt. I saw you fall. I saw you fall down this hole. I came to help," Huck said.

"Oh. Do I need help? Hmm."

"Where are we?" Huck asked.

"Wonderland. I've been here before. Why am I back?"

"'Cause you jumped down a hole," Huck said.

"There is that." Alice spotted a note. She picked it up. "It's from the queen. Not good. She's taken the long As from English. She locked them in boxes. I'm here to find the keys to the boxes and save English."

"What's a long A?"

"The long a. Sounds that say the long a. It's the way we spell words that say the ay sound. Look she left a chart. We'll have to move through each one. I guess we are looking for keys. Ready?"

"Ready.

Which Long /a/ Do I Use?

Is there more than one syllable?	"a_e" Examples: cake, same, behave	1 syllable words are very common
Is there a base word?	just "a" Examples table, acorn, baby	open syllables, can be one syllable but is usually two syllables
Where is the long a sound?	"ai" Examples: rain, sail, afraid	beginning or middle of a base word
	"ay" Examples: play, say, away	end of one syllable word
Could a word be one of those rare long spellings (ey, ei, ea)?	"ey", "eigh", "ei" they, sleight, beige, steak	very rare

Name: _____

Unlock the Long a Sound - Challenge: 1: "a_e"

Alice and Huck find White Rabbit. They show him the note.

"Oh, this is bad. This is bad indeed," Rabbit says. He looks at his watch. "But I'm late. No time to help. I found this. Now I know what it means. You fix it."

He tosses a box to Alice. He runs off. The box is locked. A note is tied to it.

"Oh!"

"What does it say?" asks Huck.

The only way to save the Long A is to solve my five puzzles. Each puzzle will get you a key. I know you can't. English will be my way forever! No more cake! No more trains. Here's your first puzzle. If you find all of the "a_e" words – you can have this pattern back. If not – no cake for you!

Signed,
The Queen of Hearts.

```
T R H I S I S G A P H T
G A T E O N N A M E I A
C K S R U M L M E T H L
A E L L F A T E N E W E
T O K N O Z E S U P E R
C L W A K E I F W A D E
R A G I L I S C T I C M
A K A L E K B A S E M E
S A L L E F O K O C O U
A S I F C A S E Y O U S
V A Y I T M I T L O U D
E E T A P E N O B A K E
U G H Y O U L W I L L A
L A K E S O U A G A V E
```

Word Bank

base	cake
case	fame
fate	game
maze	name
tale	tape
wake	gate
rate	rake
bake	lake
kale	gave
wade	save

RULE

If the letter 'a' comes before a consonant and then the letter 'e' comes at the end of the word, then the letter 'a' makes a long sound. The letter e is silent. For example, ate, ape, make, erase.

Two Pencils and a Book

Bring your completed puzzle to the puzzle master.

Name: _____

Unlock the Long a Sound - Challenge: 1: "a_e"

Alice and Huck find White Rabbit. They show him the note.

"Oh, this is bad. This is bad indeed," Rabbit says. He looks at his watch. "But I'm late. No time to help. I found this. Now I know what it means. You fix it."

He tosses a box to Alice. He runs off. The box is locked. A note is tied to it.

"Oh!"

"What does it say?" asks Huck.

```
T R H I S I S G A P H T
G A T E O N N A M E I A
C K S R U M L M E T H L
A E L L F A T E N E W E
T O K N O Z E S U P E R
C L W A K E I F W A D E
R A G I L I S C T I C M
A K A L E K B A S E M E
S A L L E F O K O C O U
A S I F C A S E Y O U S
V A Y I T M I T L O U D
E E T A P E N O B A K E
U G H Y O U L W I L L A
L A K E S O U A G A V E
```

The only way to save the Long A is to solve my five puzzles. I know you can't. English will be my way forever! No more cake with this one! Here's your first puzzle. If you find all of the "a_e" words – you can have this pattern back. If not – no cake for you!

Signed,
The Queen of Hearts.

RULE

If the letter 'a' comes before a consonant and then the letter 'e' comes at the end of the word, then the letter 'a' makes a long sound. The letter e is silent. For example, ate, ape, make, erase.

Bring your completed puzzle to the puzzle master.

Name: _____

Unlock the Long a Sound - Challenge: 1: "a_e"

Alice and Huck find White Rabbit. They show him the note.

"Oh, this is bad. This is bad indeed," Rabbit says. He looks at his watch. "But I'm late. No time to help. I found this. Now I know what it means. You fix it."

He tosses a box to Alice. He runs off. The box is locked. A note is tied to it.

"Oh!"

"What does it say?" asks Huck.

> The only way to save the Long A is to solve my five puzzles. Each puzzle will get you a key. I know you can't. English will be my way forever! No more cake! No more trains. Here's your first puzzle. If you find all of the "a_e" words – you can have this pattern back. If not – no cake for you!
>
> Signed,
> The Queen of Hearts.

```
R                    G              T
G A T E        N A M E        A
  K                M   M            L
  E            F A T E        E
               Z
      W A K E              W A D E
                    C
      K A L E        B A S E
S                F       K
A                C A S E
V                M
E     T A P E              B A K E

L A K E                    G A V E
```

Word Bank

amaze	awake
blade	blame
brave	chase
crate	craze
flake	flame
frame	grade
grape	graze
plane	plate
quake	shade
grave	slate
spade	state
trade	scale

RULE

If the letter 'a' comes before a consonant and then the letter 'e' comes at the end of the word, then the letter 'a' makes a long sound. The letter e is silent. For example, ate, ape, make, erase.

Bring your completed puzzle to the puzzle master.

Unlock the Long a Sound - Challenge: 1: "a_e"

Alice and Huck find White Rabbit. They show him the note.

"Oh, this is bad. This is bad indeed," Rabbit says. He looks at his watch. "But I'm late. No time to help. I found this. Now I know what it means. You fix it."

He tosses a box to Alice. He runs off. The box is locked. A note is tied to it.

"Oh!"

"What does it say?" asks Huck.

```
S P A D E I K N O W Y G O U
T I W A S L A T E L K R E D
A W I T H Y H O U G R A V E
T O Q U A K E N C R E D U P
E O N A D D R F L A K E E A
M H A K E U N R A P N A M B
H E R E I T S A M E Y F A R
V O P L A T E M R I T B E A
Y O L U S E M E N E W L H V
G R A Z E H E N S A M A Z E
S G N H S L A T E W G D E B
S G E H N M E C H A S E E T
S P R T R A D E I K N C E Q
M H A C H C R A T E M I N G
C R A Z E H I M T H R E E S
```

The only way to save the Long A is to solve my five puzzles. Each puzzle will get you a key. I know you can't. English will be my way forever! No more cake! No more trains. Here's your first puzzle. If you find all of the "a_e" words – you can have this pattern back. If not – no cake for you!

Signed,
The Queen of Hearts.

Word Bank

amaze	awake
blade	blame
brave	chase
crate	craze
flake	flame
frame	grade
grape	graze
plane	plate
quake	shade
grave	slate
spade	state
trade	scale

RULE

If the letter 'a' comes before a consonant and then the letter 'e' comes at the end of the word, then the letter 'a' makes a long sound. The letter e is silent. For example, ate, ape, make, erase.

Name: _____

Unlock the Long a Sound - Challenge: 1: "a_e"

Alice and Huck find White Rabbit. They show him the note.

"Oh, this is bad. This is bad indeed," Rabbit says. He looks at his watch. "But I'm late. No time to help. I found this. Now I know what it means. You fix it."

He tosses a box to Alice. He runs off. The box is locked. A note is tied to it.

"Oh!"

"What does it say?" asks Huck.

```
S P A D E I K N O W Y G O U
T I W A S L A T E L K R E D
A W I T H Y H O U G R A V E
T O Q U A K E N C R E D U P
E O N A D D R F L A K E E A
M H A K E U N R A P N A M B
H E R E I T S A M E Y F A R
V O P L A T E M R I T B E A
Y O L U S E M E N E W L H V
G R A Z E H E N S A M A Z E
S G N H S L A T E W G D E B
S G E H N M E C H A S E E T
S P R T R A D E I K N C E Q
M H A C H C R A T E M I N G
C R A Z E H I M T H R E E S
```

The only way to save the Long A is to solve my five puzzles. Each puzzle will get you a key. I know you can't. English will be my way forever! No more cake! No more trains. Here's your first puzzle. If you find all of the "a_e" words – you can have this pattern back. If not – no cake for you!

Signed,
The Queen of Hearts.

RULE

If the letter 'a' comes before a consonant and then the letter 'e' comes at the end of the word, then the letter 'a' makes a long sound. The letter e is silent. For example, ate, ape, make, erase.

Bring your completed puzzle to the puzzle master.

Name: _____

Unlock the Long a Sound - Challenge: 1: "a_e"

Alice and Huck find White Rabbit. They show him the note.

"Oh, this is bad. This is bad indeed," Rabbit says. He looks at his watch. "But I'm late. No time to help. I found this. Now I know what it means. You fix it."

He tosses a box to Alice. He runs off. The box is locked. A note is tied to it.

"Oh!"

"What does it say?" asks Huck.

```
S  P  A  D  E                          G
T           S  L  A  T  E              R
A           H              G  R  A  V  E
T     Q  U  A  K  E           R     D
E           D        F  L  A  K  E
            E        R     P        B
                     A     E        R
      P  L  A  T  E  M           B  A
      L              E           L  V
G  R  A  Z  E              A  M  A  Z  E
      N     S  L  A  T  E  W     D
      E           C  H  A  S  E
         T  R  A  D  E     K
         C  R  A  T  E
C  R  A  Z  E
```

The only way to save the Long A is to solve my five puzzles. Each puzzle will get you a key. I know you can't. English will be my way forever! No more cake! No more trains. Here's your first puzzle. If you find all of the "a_e" words — you can have this pattern back. If not — no cake for you!

Signed,
The Queen of Hearts.

Word Bank

amaze	awake
blade	blame
brave	chase
crate	craze
flake	flame
frame	grade
grape	graze
plane	plate
quake	shade
grave	slate
spade	state
trade	scale

RULE

If the letter 'a' comes before a consonant and then the letter 'e' comes at the end of the word, then the letter 'a' makes a long sound. The letter e is silent. For example, ate, ape, make, erase.

Bring your completed puzzle to the puzzle master.

Name: _____

Unlock the Long a Sound - Challenge: 1: "a_e"

Alice and Huck find White Rabbit. They show him the note.

"Oh, this is bad. This is bad indeed," Rabbit says. He looks at his watch. "But I'm late. No time to help. I found this. Now I know what it means. You fix it."

He tosses a box to Alice. He runs off. The box is locked. A note is tied to it.

"Oh!"

"What does it say?" asks Huck.

```
E D U C A T E S A T U R A D
Y I C R P A R A D E S A H E
M I S T A K E H E D Y O U F
P R E L A T E S U N D A Y L
C W M H A T S T H E M A T A
F T B E L R I N V A D E C T
O C R E O I N T H E M N I E
R D A D C L E O F T H R E N
G I C G A H I T B E C A M E
A I E S T O N M E P E G E S
V O P L E X H A H E I E T C
E B L O N D A O A V E R B A
L U E G O O L D V N I G H P
T I N S A N E M E S T A T E
A N G E C E L E B R A T E L
```

The only way to save the Long A is to solve my five puzzles. Each puzzle will get you a key. I know you can't. English will be my way forever! No more cake! No more trains. Here's your first puzzle. If you find all of the "a_e" words – you can have this pattern back. If not – no cake for you!

Signed,
The Queen of Hearts.

Word Bank

became	behave
engage	enrage
escape	estate
exhale	inhale
insane	invade
locate	parade
relate	deflate
educate	embrace
forgave	inflate
mistake	celebrate

RULE

If the letter 'a' comes before a consonant and then the letter 'e' comes at the end of the word, then the letter 'a' makes a long sound. The letter e is silent. For example, ate, ape, make, erase.

Bring your completed puzzle to the puzzle master.

Name: _____

Unlock the Long a Sound - Challenge: 1: "a_e"

Alice and Huck find White Rabbit. They show him the note.

"Oh, this is bad. This is bad indeed," Rabbit says. He looks at his watch. "But I'm late. No time to help. I found this. Now I know what it means. You fix it."

He tosses a box to Alice. He runs off. The box is locked. A note is tied to it.

"Oh!"

"What does it say?" asks Huck.

```
E D U C A T E S A T U R A D
Y I C R P A R A D E S A H E
M I S T A K E H E D Y O U F
P R E L A T E S U N D A Y L
C W M H A T S T H E M A T A
F T B E L R I N V A D E C T
O C R E O I N T H E M N I E
R D A D C L E O F T H R E N
G I C G A H I T B E C A M E
A I E S T O N M E P E G E S
V O P L E X H A H E I E T C
E B L O N D A O A V E R B A
L U E G O O L D V N I G H P
T I N S A N E M E S T A T E
A N G E C E L E B R A T E L
```

The only way to save the Long A is to solve my five puzzles. Each puzzle will get you a key. I know you can't. English will be my way forever! No more cake! No more trains. Here's your first puzzle. If you find all of the "a_e" words - you can have this pattern back. If not - no cake for you!

Signed,
The Queen of Hearts.

RULE

If the letter 'a' comes before a consonant and then the letter 'e' comes at the end of the word, then the letter 'a' makes a long sound. The letter e is silent. For example, ate, ape, make, erase.

Bring your completed puzzle to the puzzle master.

Name: _____

Unlock the Long a Sound - Challenge: 1: "a_e"

Alice and Huck find White Rabbit. They show him the note.

"Oh, this is bad. This is bad indeed," Rabbit says. He looks at his watch. "But I'm late. No time to help. I found this. Now I know what it means. You fix it."

He tosses a box to Alice. He runs off. The box is locked. A note is tied to it.

"Oh!"

"What does it say?" asks Huck.

The only way to save the Long A is to solve my five puzzles. Each puzzle will get you a key. I know you can't. English will be my way forever! No more cake! No more trains. Here's your first puzzle. If you find all of the "a_e" words – you can have this pattern back. If not – no cake for you!

Signed,
The Queen of Hearts.

```
E D U C A T E                    D
        P A R A D E              E
M I S T A K E                    F
    R E L A T E                  L
    M                            A
F   B   L       I N V A D E      T
O   R   O               N        E
R   A   C               R
G   A   C   I     B E C A M E
A   E   A   N     E       G     S
V       T   N     E       E     C
E       E X H A H E     E       A
            A   A               P
            L   V               E
  I N S A N E     E S T A T E
      C E L E B R A T E
```

Word Bank

became	behave
engage	enrage
escape	estate
exhale	inhale
insane	invade
locate	parade
relate	deflate
educate	embrace
forgave	inflate
mistake	celebrate

RULE

If the letter 'a' comes before a consonant and then the letter 'e' comes at the end of the word, then the letter 'a' makes a long sound. The letter e is silent. For example, ate, ape, make, erase.

Bring your completed puzzle to the puzzle master.

Unlock the Long a Sound - Challenge: 2 "ai"

"We did it. We got the first key."

A tea table pops up. It seems to come from no where.

"Of course there are more," says Hatter.

"Hello old friend," says Alice. "We're here to…"

"I know why you're here. I have a note. Or I had a note. I lost it. It said to find the "ai" long a words," Hatter says. "But I still have this box."

"What's that rule?" asks Huck

"We use "ai" in the middle of words. Think rain, pail, train," Alice says. "What else did it say?"

"It said to bring back the "ai" long a sound, we have to find the message hidden in the reading. We have to find the blocked-out letters. Then unscramble them to make a sentence."

"Let's do it," says Huck.

Mark went out to pla▮ but the rain came down. He ran to the main ro▮d and hid under a big tree. His ▮hirt got a big stain. Mark felt a pain in his foot. He wanted to gain sp▮ed to ▮each home f▮st.

On the way, he saw a train. ▮he train made a l▮ud noise as it went by. Mark saw paint on a wall. ▮t was still wet and looked nice.

He had ▮o wait for the rain to stop. Near him was a snail. The snail was not afraid of ▮he rain. It moved slow ▮ut had a ▮oal. Mark wanted to be like the snail.

Then, the rai▮ started to drain ▮way. Mark ▮ould go home now. He took aim and ran fast. Mark was always fait▮ful to get home on tim▮. He d▮d not want to fail.

At home, Mar▮ was happy. He had p▮id attention and made it home safe.

___ ___ Y ___ ___ ___ ___ N

___ ___ ___ E ___ ___ ___ ___

___ ___ ___ ___ ___ C ___ ___ ___

Name: _____

Unlock the Long a Sound - Challenge: 2 "ai"

"We did it. We got the first key."

A tea table pops up. It seems to come from no where.

"Of course there are more," says Hatter.

"Hello old friend," says Alice. "We're here to…"

"I know why you're here. I have a note. Or I had a note. I lost it. It said to find the "ai" long a words," Hatter says. "But I still have this box."

"What's that rule?" asks Huck

"We use "ai" in the middle of words. Think rain, pail, train," Alice says. "What else did it say?"

"It said to bring back the "ai" long a sound, we have to find the message hidden in the reading. We have to find the blocked-out letters. Then unscramble them to make a sentence."

"Let's do it," says Huck.

Mark went out to pla◯ but the rain came down. He ran to the main ro◯d and hid under a big tree. His ◯hirt got a big stain. Mark felt a pain in his foot. He wanted to gain sp◯ed to ◯each home f◯st.

On the way, he saw a train. ◯he train made a l◯ud noise as it went by. Mark saw paint on a wall. ◯t was still wet and looked nice.

He had ◯o wait for the rain to stop. Near him was a snail. The snail was not afraid of ◯he rain. It moved slow ◯ut had a ◯oal. Mark wanted to be like the snail.

Then, the rai◯ started to drain ◯way. Mark ◯ould go home now. He took aim and ran fast. Mark was always fait◯ful to get home on tim◯. He d◯d not want to fail.

At home, Mar◯ was happy. He had p◯id attention and made it home safe.

___ ___ ___ ___   ___ ___ ___ ___

___ ___   ___ ___ ___ ___   ___ ___ ___ ___

___ ___   ___ ___ ___ ___

Bring your completed puzzle to the puzzle master.

Name: _____

Unlock the Long a Sound - Challenge: 2 "ai"

"We did it. We got the first key."

A tea table pops up. It seems to come from no where.

"Of course there are more," says Hatter.

"Hello old friend," says Alice. "We're here to…"

"I know why you're here. I have a note. Or I had a note. I lost it. It said to find the "ai" long a words," Hatter says. "But I still have this box."

"What's that rule?" asks Huck

"We use "ai" in the middle of words. Think rain, pail, train," Alice says. "What else did it say?"

"It said to bring back the "ai" long a sound, we have to find the message hidden in the reading. We have to find the blocked-out letters. Then unscramble them to make a sentence."

"Let's do it," says Huck.

Mark went out to play but the rain came down. He ran to the main road and hid under a big tree. His shirt got a big stain. Mark felt a pain in his foot. He wanted to gain speed to reach home first.

On the way, he saw a train. The train made a loud noise as it went by. Mark saw paint on a wall. It was still wet and looked nice.

He had to wait for the rain to stop. Near him was a snail. The snail was not afraid of the rain. It moved slow but had a goal. Mark wanted to be like the snail.

Then, the rain started to drain away. Mark could go home now. He took aim and ran fast. Mark was always faithful to get home on time. He did not want to fail.

At home, Mark was happy. He had paid attention and made it home safe.

___ SAY ___   ___ ___ RAIN

___ TO ___   ___ ___ GET   ___ ___ THE

___ AI   ___ BACK ___

Unlock the Long a Sound - Challenge: 3: "ay"

Next, Alice and Huck run into the Caterpillar. It's up in a tree.

"I've been waiting," it says slowly.

"Will you help us bring back long a?" asks Alice.

"Figure out the message and the long "ay" sound will come back," it says. A box appears.

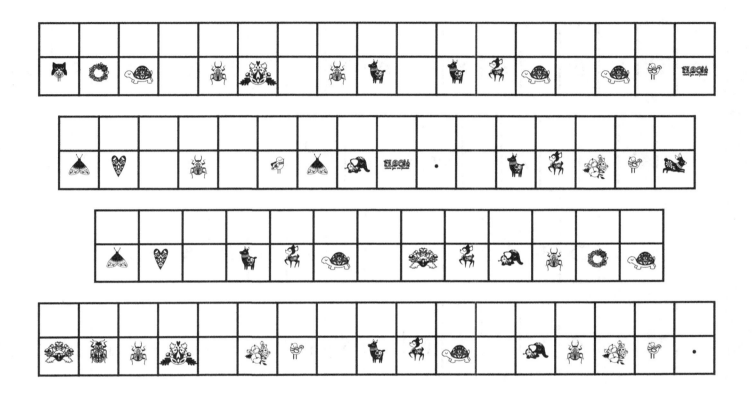

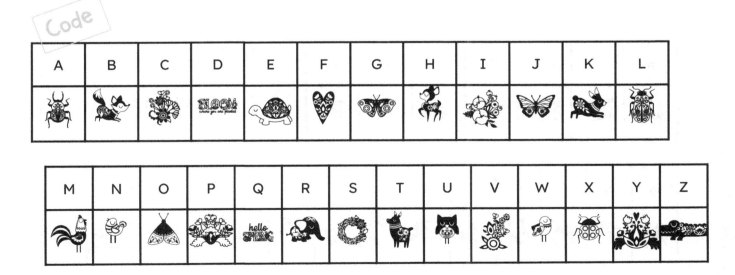

Bring your completed puzzle to the puzzle master.

Bring your completed puzzle to the puzzle master.

Name: _____

Unlock the Long a Sound - Challenge: 3: "ay"

Next, Alice and Huck run into the Caterpillar. It's up in a tree.

"I've been waiting," it says slowly.

"Will you help us bring back long a?" asks Alice.

"Figure out the message and the long "ay" sound will come back," it says. A box appears.

| U | S | E | | A | Y | | A | T | | T | H | E | | E | N | D |

| O | F | | A | | W | O | R | D | . | | T | H | I | N | K |

| O | F | | T | H | E | | P | H | R | A | S | E |

| P | L | A | Y | | I | N | | T | H | E | | R | A | I | N | . |

Code

A	B	C	D	E	F	G	H	I	J	K	L

M	N	O	P	Q	R	S	T	U	V	W	X	Y	Z

Bring your completed puzzle to the puzzle master.

Unlock the Long a Sound - Challenge: 4: "eigh"

"Look," Huck points to the sky. A plane had written – NO! You are too close!

"That's odd," says Alice.

"Sure is. Planes aren't even a thing yet."

"Looks like we're winning," Alice says.

"You are," says the Cheshire Cat. He was in a tree.

"Hello," says Alice.

"I have a note for you," the cat says. Then it disappears. In its place – a box.

Three down. But there won't be more. This puzzle is much harder. It is a word search puzzle with a hidden message in it. First, find all of the words that are underlined in the reading. The leftover letters form a message. You'll never get it. Ha!

Signed,
The Queen

Jane has eight new books. She puts them in a box. The box has a weight on it. The weight is not too heavy.

It was cold, so Jane went on a sleigh ride. The sleigh went fast in the snow. Jane saw her neighbors. They waved and said hello.

Jane's neighbors are nice. They are very neighborly. They help Jane when she needs it.

Jane likes to watch a weightlifter. He can lift a big weight. It is very weighty.

The weightlifter is eighteen years old. He was born in the eighties. He is as tall as his height allows.

Jane hears a loud neigh. It is from a horse near the freight. The freight train passes by her house.

Jane smiles. She likes her quiet street and her good neighbors.

```
S  L  E  I  G  H  I  T  E  I  G  H
W  E  I  G  H  T  L  I  F  T  E  R
N  E  I  G  H  I  S  W  A  V  E  D
B  O  X  W  E  I  G  H  T  Y  I  S
O  N  B  O  R  N  L  Y  T  A  L  L
U  N  E  I  G  H  B  O  R  S  S  E
D  N  E  A  R  A  T  T  H  E  E  N
D  B  Y  O  F  H  E  I  G  H  T  A
S  A  I  D  W  O  I  N  R  D  A  S
B  E  H  E  R  F  O  R  E  T  O  N
```

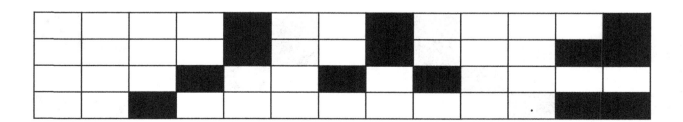

Unlock the Long a Sound - Challenge: 4: "eigh"

"Look," Huck points to the sky. A plane had written – NO! You are too close!

"That's odd," says Alice.

"Sure is. Planes aren't even a thing yet."

"Looks like we're winning," Alice says.

"You are," says the Cheshire Cat. He was in a tree.

"Hello," says Alice.

"I have a note for you," the cat says. Then it disappears. In its place – a box.

Three down. But there won't be more. This puzzle is much harder. It is a word search puzzle with a hidden message in it. First, find all of the words that are underlined in the reading. The leftover letters form a message. You'll never get it. Ha!

Signed,
The Queen

Jane has eight new books. She puts them in a box. The <u>box</u> has a weight <u>on</u> it. The weight <u>is</u> not too heavy.

<u>It</u> was cold, so Jane went on a sleigh ride. The <u>sleigh</u> went fast <u>in</u> the snow. Jane saw her neighbors. They <u>waved</u> and <u>said</u> hello.

Jane's neighbors are nice. They are very neighborly. They help Jane when she needs it.

Jane likes to watch a weightlifter. He can lift a big weight. It is very <u>weighty</u>.

The weightlifter is eighteen years old. He was <u>born</u> in the eighties. He is as <u>tall as</u> his <u>height</u> allows.

Jane hears a loud <u>neigh</u>. It is from a horse <u>near</u> the freight. The freight train passes <u>by</u> her house.

Jane smiles. She likes <u>her</u> quiet street and her good <u>neighbors</u>.

S	L	E	I	G	H	I	T	E	I	G	H
W	E	I	G	H	T	L	I	F	T	E	R
N	E	I	G	H	I	S	W	A	V	E	D
B	O	X	W	E	I	G	H	T	Y	I	S
O	N	B	O	R	N	L	Y	T	A	L	L
U	N	E	I	G	H	B	O	R	S	S	E
D	N	E	A	R	A	T	T	H	E	E	N
D	B	Y	O	F	H	E	I	G	H	T	A
S	A	I	D	W	O	I	N	R	D	A	S
B	E	H	E	R	F	O	R	E	T	O	N

			H						O		
			D		A					E	
		D					A			R	
	R		B						.		

Name: _____

Unlock the Long a Sound - Challenge: 4: "eigh"

"Look," Huck points to the sky. A plane had written – NO! You are too close!

"That's odd," says Alice.

"Sure is. Planes aren't even a thing yet."

"Looks like we're winning," Alice says.

"You are," says the Cheshire Cat. He was in a tree.

"Hello," says Alice.

"I have a note for you," the cat says. Then it disappears. In its place – a box.

Three down. But there won't be more. This puzzle is much harder. It is a word search puzzle with a hidden message in it. First, find all of the words that are underlined in the reading. The leftover letters form a message. You'll never get it. Ha!

Signed,
The Queen

Jane has eight new books. She puts them in a box. The box has a weight on it. The weight is not too heavy.

It was cold, so Jane went on a sleigh ride. The sleigh went fast in the snow. Jane saw her neighbors. They waved and said hello.

Jane's neighbors are nice. They are very neighborly. They help Jane when she needs it.

Jane likes to watch a weightlifter. He can lift a big weight. It is very weighty.

The weightlifter is eighteen years old. He was born in the eighties. He is as tall as his height allows.

Jane hears a loud neigh. It is from a horse near the freight. The freight train passes by her house.

Jane smiles. She likes her quiet street and her good neighbors.

```
S  L  E  I  G  H  I  T  E  I  G  H
W  E  I  G  H  T  L  I  F  T  E  R
N  E  I  G  H  I  S  W  A  V  E  D
B  O  X  W  E  I  G  H  T  Y  I  S
O  N  B  O  R  N  L  Y  T  A  L  L
U  N  E  I  G  H  B  O  R  S  S  E
D  N  E  A  R  A  T  T  H  E  E  N
D  B  Y  O  F  H  E  I  G  H  T  A
S  A  I  D  W  O  I  N  R  D  A  S
B  E  H  E  R  F  O  R  E  T  O  N
```

E	I	G	H		I	S		O	N	L	Y	
U	S	E	D		A	T		T	H	E		
E	N	D		O	F		A		W	O	R	D
O	R		B	E	F	O	R	E	T	.		

Bring your completed puzzle to the puzzle master.

Unlock the Long a Sound - Challenge: 5: Long a

"The key appeared with this note," Alice says.

"No more odd Wonderland people?" Huck asks.

"Oh yes. There are more. But now now. It says we must solve the puzzle. Then we'll get the location of the last key. It's a logic puzzle. We have to match the word with its pattern and where the Queen hid them."

"You mean the Queen hid all of the long a words?" Huck asks.

"Looks like it. Let's get going. It's almost time for tea."

		Vowel Team					Hiding Place				
		a_e	Just "a"	"ai"	"ay"	"eigh"	Oak Tree	Barn	In the tulips	Rabbit hole	By the lake
Word	weigh										
	baby										
	train										
	cake										
	play										
Hiding Pace	Oak tree										
	Barn										
	In the tulips										
	Rabbit hole										
	By the lake										

Clues

1. Match the word with its spelling pattern.
2. Neither "a_e" words and the "ai" words are in the oak tree, in the barn or by the lake.
3. The "ay" words are in a hiding place with the a_e pattern.
4. The a_e words are underground.
5. The "just a" words are not in the barn.

Bring your completed puzzle to the puzzle master.

Unlock the Long a Sound - Challenge: 5: Long a

"The key appeared with this note," Alice says.

"No more odd Wonderland people?" Huck asks.

"Oh yes. There are more. But now now. It says we must solve the puzzle. Then we'll get the location of the last key. It's a logic puzzle. We have to match the word with its pattern and where the Queen hid them."

"You mean the Queen hid all of the long a words?" Huck asks.

"Looks like it. Let's get going. It's almost time for tea."

		Vowel Team					Hiding Place				
		a_e	Just "a"	"ai"	"ay"	"eigh"	Oak Tree	Barn	In the tulips	Rabbit hole	By the lake
Word	weigh	X	X	X	X	O	X	O	X	X	X
	baby	X	O	X	X	X	O	X	X	X	X
	train	X	X	O	X	X	X	X	O	X	X
	cake	O	X	X	X	X	X	X	X	O	X
	play	X	X	X	O	X	X	X	X	X	O
Hiding Pace	Oak tree	X	O	X	X	X					
	Barn	X	X	X	X	O					
	In the tulips	X	X	O	X	X					
	Rabbit hole	O	X	X	X	X					
	By the lake	X	X	X	O	X					

Clues

1. Match the word with its spelling pattern.
2. Neither "a_e" words and the "ai" words are in the oak tree, in the barn or by the lake.
3. The "ay" words are in a hiding place with the a_e pattern.
4. The a_e words are underground.
5. The "just a" words are not in the barn.

Bring your completed puzzle to the puzzle master.

You Did It!
You beat the Queen of Hearts and have restored the Long A sound back English.

Long "a" Puzzle 1 Winner **Long**	Long "a" Puzzle 2 Winner **Long**
Long "a" Puzzle 2 Winner **"a"**	Long "a" Puzzle 2 Winner **"a"**
Long "a" Puzzle 3 Winner **is**	Long "a" Puzzle 3 Winner **is**
Long "a" Puzzle 4 Winner **the**	Long "a" Puzzle 4 Winner **the**
Long "a" Puzzle 5 Winner **way**	Long "a" Puzzle 5 Winner **way**

Fluency Tracker

Name: _____ Period: _____

Passage #	Date	CWPM	Date	CWPM	Date	CWPM

Fluency Chart

Name: _____ Period: _____

Correct Words Per Minute																								
115																								
110																								
105																								
100																								
95																								
90																								
85																								
80																								
75																								
70																								
65																								
60																								
55																								
50																								
45																								
40																								
35																								
30																								
25																								
20																								
15																								
10																								
5																								
Date																								
Passage Title																								

Research

Abbott, M., Wills, H., Miller, A., & Kaufman, J. (2012). The relationship of error rate and comprehension in second and third grade oral reading fluency. Reading Psychology, 33(1–2), 104–132.

Chard, D. J., Vaughn, S., & Tyler, B. J. (2002). A synthesis of research on effective interventions for building reading fluency with elementary students with learning disabilities. Journal of Learning Disabilities, 35(5), 386–406.

Chomsky, C. (1976). After decoding: What? Language Arts, 53(3), 288–296.

Deno, S. L., Mirkin, P. K., & Chiang, B. (1982). Identifying valid measures of reading. Exceptional Children, 49, 36-43.

Deno, S. (2003). Developments in curriculum-based measurement. The Journal of Special Education, 37, 184-192. doi:10.1177/00224669030370030801 http://digitalcommons.unl.edu/buroscurriculum/3.

Eldredge, J. L., & Quinn, D. W. (1988). Increasing reading performance of low-achieving second graders with dyad reading groups. Journal of Educational Research, 82(1), 40–46.

Fuchs, L. S., Fuchs, D., Hamlett, C. L., Walz, L., & Germann, G. (1993). Formative evaluation of academic progress: How much growth can we expect? School Psychology Review, 22(1), 27–48.

Fuchs, L. S., Fuchs, D., Hamlett, C. L., & Whinnery, K. (1991). Effects of goal line feedback on level, slope, and stability of performance within curriculum-based measurement. Learning Disabilities Research and Practice, 6(2), 66–74.

Fuchs, L. S., Fuchs, D., Hosp, M. K., & Jenkins, J. R. (2001). Oral reading fluency as an indicator of reading competence: A theoretical, empirical, and historical analysis. Scientific Studies of Reading, 5(3), 239–256.

Hasbrouck, J., & Tindal, G (2005). Oral reading fluency: 90 years of measurement (Tech. Rep. No. 33, Behavioral Research and Teaching (BRT)). University of Oregon, College of Education.

Hasbrouck, J., & Tindal, G. A. (2006). Oral reading fluency norms: A valuable assessment tool for reading teachers. The Reading Teacher. 59(7),636–644.

Hasbrouck, J., & Tindal, G. (2017). An update to the compiled ORF norms (Technical Report No. 1702). Eugene, OR: Behavioral Research and Teaching, University of Oregon.

Heckelman, R. G. (1969). A neurological-impress method of remedial-reading instruction. Academic Therapy Quarterly, 5(4), 277–282.

Klauda, S. L., & Guthrie, J. T. (2008). Relationships of three components of reading fluency to reading comprehension. Journal of Educational Psychology, 100(2), 310–321.

Kim, Y., Petscher, Y., Schatschneider, C., & Foorman, B. (2010). Does growth rate in oral reading fluency matter in predicting reading comprehension achievement? Journal of Educational Psychology, 102(3), 652–667.

Kuhn, M. R., Schwanenflugel, P. J., & Meisinger, E. B. (2010). Aligning theory and assessment of reading fluency: Automaticity, prosody, and definitions of fluency. Reading Research Quarterly, 45(2), 230–251.

Kuhn, M. R., & Stahl, S. A. (2003). Fluency: A review of developmental and remedial practices. Journal of Educational Psychology, 95(1), 3–21.

LaBerge, D., & Samuels, S. J. (1974). Toward a theory of automatic information processing in reading. Cognitive Psychology, 6(2), 292–323.

Lee, J., & Yoon Yoon, S. (2015). The effects of repeated reading on reading fluency for students with reading disabilities: A meta-analysis. Journal of Learning Disabilities, 50(2), 213–224.

Morgan, P. L., & Sideridis, G. D. (2006). Contrasting the effectiveness of fluency interventions for students with or at risk for learning disabilities: A multilevel random coefficient modeling metaanalysis. Learning Disabilities Research & Practice, 21(4), 191–210.

Morgan, P. L., Sideridis, G., & Hua, Y. (2011). Initial and over-time effects of fluency interventions for students with or at risk for disabilities. The Journal of Special Education, 46(2), 94–116.

National Institute of Child Health and Human Development. (2000a). Report of the National Reading Panel. Teaching children to read: An evidence-based assessment of the scientific research literature on reading and its implications for reading instruction (NIH Publication No. 00-4769). Washington, DC: U.S. Government Printing Office.

National Institute of Child Health and Human Development. (2000b). Report of the National Reading Panel. Teaching children to read: An evidence-based assessment of the scientific research literature on reading and its implications for reading instruction: Reports of the subgroups (NIH Publication No. 00-4754). Washington, DC: U.S. Government Printing Office.

Price, K. W., Meisinger, E. B., Louwerse, M. M., & D'Mello, S. (2015). The contributions of oral and silent reading fluency to reading comprehension. Reading Psychology, 37(2), 167–201.

Prior, S. M., Fenwick, K. D., Saunders, K.S., Ouellette, R., O'Quinn, C., & Harney, S. (2011). Comprehension after oral and silent reading: Does grade level matter? Literacy Research and Instruction, 50(3), 183–194.

Reutzel, D. R., & Hollingsworth, P. M. (1993). Effects of fluency training on second graders' reading comprehension. Journal of Educational Research, 86(6), 325–331.

Schwanenflugel, P. J., Meisinger, E. B., Wisenbaker, J. M., Kuhn, M. R., Strauss, G. P., Morris, R. D. (2006). Becoming a fluent and automatic reader in the early elementary school years. Reading Research Quarterly, 41(4), 496–522.

Therrien, W. J. (2004). Fluency and comprehension gains as a result of repeated reading. Remedial and Special Education, 25(4), 252–261.

Williamson, G.L. (2004). Student readiness for postsecondary options. Durham, NC: MetaMetrics.

Williamson, G.L. (2008). A text readability continuum for postsecondary readiness. Journal of Advanced Academics, 19 (4), 602-632.

Made in the USA
Monee, IL
24 April 2025

16310994R00116